LILLIAN
JENNIF

20

FORTUNE &
FENG SHUI
SHEEP

KONSEPBOOKS
ASTROLOGY . FENG SHUI . INSPIRATIONS

Congratulations!

Hi there!

Firstly, I want to thank and congratulate you for investing in yourself... and the latest edition of Fortune and Feng Shui... your personalized horoscope book for 2012! Today you have purchased one of the best possible books on the market today to guide and help you safely through the upcoming year!

What will you be earning one year from today? How will you look and feel... will you be happier and healthier in 2012?

In this little book, Jennifer and I reveal many insights pertaining to your particular animal sign...what you can expect and how to protect and enhance all areas of your life for success in 2012.

But Why Stop Here?

Now you can discover other powerful feng shui secrets from me that go hand-in-hand with the valuable information in this book. And it's absolutely FREE!

My Personal Invitation

I'd like to extend my personal invitation to you to receive my FREE online weekly newsletter… Lillian Too's Mandala Ezine. You took the first positive step to success when you purchased this book. Now you can expand your wealth luck and knowledge…and learn more about authentic feng shui that really works… including the all-important 3rd dimension of spiritual feng shui when you sign up for my FREE newsletter.

Just go to *www.lilliantoomandalaezine.com* and register today! My ezine will be delivered to your inbox each week loaded with great feng shui articles, hints and tips to make 2012 your best year ever.

IT'S EASY! IT'S FREE! IT'S FRESH
AND NEW EACH WEEK!

Don't miss out! It's easy to register at *www.lilliantoomandalaezine.com* and you'll also receive a special BONUS from me when you register today!

All the best,
Lillian

P.S. Lillian's online FREE weekly ezine is only available to those who register online at *www.lilliantoomandalaezine.com*

P.P.S. Ezine subscribers also receive special offer, discounts and bonuses from me throughout the year!

Fortune & Feng Shui 2012 SHEEP
by Lillian Too and Jennifer Too
© 2012 Konsep Lagenda Sdn Bhd

Text © 2012 Lillian Too and Jennifer Too
Photographs and illustrations © WOFS.com Sdn Bhd

The moral right of the authors to be identified as authors of this book has been asserted.

Published by KONSEP LAGENDA SDN BHD (223 855)
Kuala Lumpur 59100 Malaysia

For more Konsep books, go to www.lillian-too.com or www.wofs.com
To report errors, please send a note to errors@konsepbooks.com
For general feedback, email feedback@konsepbooks.com

Notice of Rights
All rights reserved. No part of this publication may be reproduced, stored in a retrieval system or transmitted in any form, or by any means, electronic, mechanical, photocopying, recording, or otherwise, without the prior written permission of the publisher.
For information on getting permission for reprints and excerpts, contact: permissions@konsepbooks.com

Notice of Liability
The information in this book is distributed on an "As Is" basis, without warranty. While every precaution has been taken in the preparation of the book, neither the author nor Konsep Lagenda shall have any liability to any person or entity with respect to any loss or damage caused or alleged to be caused directly or indirectly by the instructions contained in this book.

ISBN 978-967-329-073-4
Published in Malaysia, August 2011

for more on all the recommended
feng shui cures, remedies & enhancers for

2012

please log on to

www.wofs.com

and

www.fsmegamall.com

SHEEP BORN CHART

BIRTH YEAR	WESTERN CALENDAR DATES	AGE	KUA NUMBER MALES	KUA NUMBER FEMALES
Metal Sheep	17 Feb 1931 to 5 Feb 1932	81	6 West Group	9 East Group
Water Sheep	5 Feb 1943 to 24 Jan 1944	69	3 East Group	3 East Group
Wood Sheep	24 Jan 1955 to 11 Feb 1956	57	9 East Group	6 West Group
Fire Sheep	9 Feb 1967 to 29 Jan 1968	45	6 West Group	9 East Group
Earth Sheep	28 Jan 1979 to 15 Feb 1980	33	3 East Group	3 East Group
Metal Sheep	15 Feb 1991 to 3 Feb 1992	21	9 East Group	6 West Group
Water Sheep	1 Feb 2003 to 21 Jan 2004	9	6 West Group	9 East Group

CONTENTS

CHAPTER 3.
Personalising Your Feng Shui Luck In 2012

Individualised Directions to Protect Your Good Feng Shui

CHAPTER 4.
Relationship Luck For 2012

The Sheep should focus on work to dispel & dissolve afflicted relationship luck

CHAPTER 5.
Analysing Your Luck In Each Month

CHAPTER 6.
Powerful Protection Of Your Luck With Tien Ti Ren

Activating The Complete Trinity Of Luck With Spiritual Feng Shui

YEAR OF THE WATER DRAGON 2012
A Transformational Year

The Sheep in 2012 enters the year with greater strength of purpose and a newfound confidence that will make the Year of the Dragon very special indeed. The Sheep has to contend with some hostile feng shui winds, but for many of you, this is also a year when there is wealth and success luck. Much of the year's energies are colored by the incredible aura of the Dragon, the Zodiac system's most powerful sign.

This is the Year of Water Dragon & it is going to be a transformational year with both positive & negative manifestations of quite extreme luck. The stars of the annual paht chee together with the patterns of element relationships bring early indications that the developments of this year will bring far-reaching and life-changing consequences to many people.

For the Sheep, the year's winds bring a new, more aggressive phase into your lives. You will be empowered and driven by the energy of the Dragon.

For some, this plays out very well indeed, taking you into a new league professionally. For others however, it could turn out to be the kind of year when even friends seem like foes. You might even find yourself in an adversarial situation with once-close colleagues and associates. This situation is very much influenced by the feng shui winds of the year's chart and by the effect of the 24 Mountain Stars impacting on you. The year's paht chee chart also adds aggressive influences that affect you as well.

First, note the **three stars** influencing the energy of the year.

The *Star of Aggressive Sword* makes an appearance, so there is a great need to be wary. Violence in the world has not abated. There continues to be an air of collective anger pervading the world's atmosphere, which continues to find an outlet.

Interestingly also, in the 2012 paht chee chart, the Tiger continues to be around and it is a strong Water Tiger that complements the year's Water Dragon. With Tiger and Dragon present, and the Rooster as well (which symbolizes the Phoenix and is the Dragon's secret friend), we see the presence of three celestial guardians as well as the powerful hand of heaven.

It is a year when destinies play out with brutal efficiency and big transformations take place. This is confirmed by the number 6 in the center of the feng shui chart. Heavenly energies rule this year.

Cosmic forces are extremely powerful in 2012 and the best way to ride the Dragon Year, the most effective way to emerge stronger and healthier, happier and richer this year, is to rely greatly on powerful cosmic guardians. And to always wear symbols of victory!

It is a year when wearing protective powerful mantras and syllables on the body can be the difference between sailing through the year safely or becoming some kind of victim.

Protective amulets should always be worn touching the energy vortexes of the throat, the heart and also near to the navel where the body's central chakra is located and where all the "winds" of the body's channels converge. Strengthening the chakras of the human body system enhances attunement to the environment. This is as true for you, as for all other signs but more you, the Sheep because you need to cope with the hostile energy caused by the feng shui affliction affecting you this year. Put on protective amulets that touch the energy vortexes of your throat, your heart and near to the navel where the body's central chakra is located and where all the "winds" of the body's channels converge. Strengthening the chakras of the human body system enhances attunement to the environment.

We are currently living through a time when the energies of the world are in a state of flux. You the Sheep must take cognizance of this and make certain you are not in the wrong place at the wrong time.

Staying protected and in sync with the disturbing energies of the environment is worth the small effort involved, especially if it can help you avoid getting inadvertently involved in a potentially violent situation.

2012 brings also the star of the *External Flower of Romance*, a star which fuels potentially painful passions. Those hit by it and engage in affairs out of wedlock are sure to create hurtful waves and aggravations in their lives! Relationship woes could well escalate in 2012; it will be worse than last year and no one is immune.

It is wise to take some strong precautions. Bring good feng shui protection into the bedroom and be particularly conscious of auspicious sleeping directions that protect the family and your marriage relationship this year. Also put into place safeguards that protect your particular love relationship.

For the ambitious and those determined to succeed, the year also brings the *Star of Powerful Mentors*.

For the Sheep in its prime i.e. the **45 year old Sheep**, your birth chart has the vital Fire element (which is missing this year) and this brings you the auspicious luck of influential people turning up in your life to give you strong and meaningful support.

In 2012, you benefit from your bosses who can act as mentor figures in your professional life. These people will support you and bring you to new heights of success. Their support could well mean the difference between failure and fabulous success.

And due to the presence of the *Mentor Star* in the year's pattern of influences, it benefits for you to activate mentor luck in your life this year.

Compass directions and locations of sleeping areas must be correctly monitored this year; and the symbol of the Crystal Globe with a Dragon perched at the top ascending towards the Universe and the skies attracts the all-important heaven luck.

We have designed a very special crystal globe to be placed in the center of homes especially for this purpose - to act as a catalyst. This **Dragon on a Crystal Globe** adds much towards enhancing the energy of the Sheep's home & work space. It helps actualize *Mentor Luck* for you!

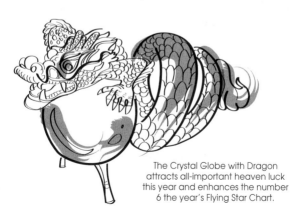

The Crystal Globe with Dragon attracts all-important heaven luck this year and enhances the number 6 the year's Flying Star Chart.

You should also take note of the luck of different months so that your luck is properly fine-tuned. Know your good months, for these are times when you can be confident and when opportunities will ripen in an auspicious manner. Troubled months are when it is advisable to refrain from making big decisions or embarking on important journeys. They are also the times to put suitable remedies in place so that whatever setbacks, illnesses or disappointments that make an appearance will be minor in nature.

This series of *Fortune & Feng Shui* books for the 12 animal signs of the Lunar Zodiac is written based on studies made into the year's Paht Chee and feng shui charts. Information in these charts are combined with Flying Star feng shui technology, 24 Mountains Compass Stars cycle and the Tibetan Wheel of Elements to bring you accurate readings on what to expect for the coming year.

We go to great lengths to analyze the charts and research the cures so that we can incorporate powerful feng shui and astrological recommendations. Our philosophy of practice is that bad luck should always be effectively averted and good luck must always be strongly activated to manifest. So these books are not mere passive readings of luck.

This year we focus on the importance of house layout design and feng shui directions as these appear to offer the best ways of taking the fullest advantage of the Dragon, Tiger and Phoenix celestial presence in the paht chee chart. This is an auspicious configuration which has the potential to channel heavenly good fortune your way.

So included within is advice about placement of symbolic objects that have a celestial connection. Placed correctly within the home, they act as catalysts to luck, thus facilitating your journey through the year, ensuring you sail through relatively trouble free.

The big thing for 2012 is the power of the Blue Dragon and the great importance of Fire energy, because Fire is missing in this year's chart. The presence of Fire will instantly improve the luck of any space. This is a year to invest in bright lights and candles.

The presence of **crystal or glass globes** and **wishgranting jewels** in the center of the home will be especially auspicious as this brings the luck of increasing wealth. In 2012, the element that signifies prosperity is the Earth element so having crystal balls on your coffee tables, especially those embellished with auspicious symbols and important sutras, are sure to offer excellent harmonious relationship luck as well as prosperity luck.

In 2012, the element that signifies *Prosperity* is the *Earth element.*

These books are meant to assist readers to understand **how their astrological and destiny luck can be improved** with good feng shui in this important transformational year of the Dragon. Recommendations are based on calculations

and interpretations of the charts, and analysis has been simplified so that the advice given is easily understood. Even those with no previous experience with feng shui or fortune enhancement practices will find it easy, fun and **ultimately very effective** using astrology and the placement of symbolic objects to improve their luck.

This book on the Sheep's fortunes for 2012 is one of twelve written specially for each Zodiac sign. It offers almost a recipe-type, easy approach to preparing for the year ahead. If you find it helpful for yourself, you might also want to monitor the luck pattern of your loved ones. Who knows how good advice given within may be just the thing to jump start their auspicious fortune, causing it to ripen!

This is a year when everything good or bad will seem to be larger than usual in magnitude and definitely transformational in effect. It is worthwhile taking some trouble to ensure that the year's energy really does sync beautifully with yours.

GENERAL OUTLOOK FOR THE YEAR

There were severe earthquakes, floods, storms, forest fires and volcanic eruptions in the past two years, creating a disaster driven scenario which last year was compounded by the severity of violence and civil conflicts in many of the world's troubled countries.

The last two years 2010 and 2011 saw troubled times brought by the clash of stem and branch elements, not just in the important year pillar, but also in all the other pillars. These paht chee chart indications brought suffering and loss on a global scale, and in the immediate past year, they manifested in different parts of the world with frightening reality. The violence that erupted in the countries of Northern Africa and the Middle East was scary, but so were city-shattering earthquakes, widespread floods, gigantic storms, volcanic eruptions and terrifying tsunamis, all of which started towards the closing months of 2010 and continuing into 2011. These seem to lend credence to the highly publicized end of the world predictions for 2012.

Yet happily, amidst all the natural disasters and violence that have occurred, those who stayed safe also went on to enjoy good times and good news. This was because the year 2011 also benefited from powerful feng shui winds and enjoyed windows of good fortune brought by quite a good number of big and small auspicious star energies from the 24 Mountain compass stars.

So although the destiny chart of elements of the past couple of years did bring turbulent times and conflicts to many parts of the world, these discordant energies told only half the story. On a micro basis many were able to seize the opportunities that manifested during the past year.

For 2012, Chinese Astrology does not predict an end of world scenario. But will we see an end to the disaster scenario of the past two years? The charts suggest a slowing down.

2012 is the year of the powerful Water Dragon, so from an element perspective it also benefits those of you born in the year of the **Wood Sheep** - for you, there is some big time wealth and success luck coming, so all you 57 year olds really have an abundant year ahead for you. Wealth luck ripens magnificently, as does success luck too!

This year is also especially beneficial for **33 year old Earth Sheep**. Your Earth element subdues the Water element of the Dragon and Earth also signifies wealth luck this year. So this will also be a year of abundance and great success for the 33 year old Earth Sheep who enjoys the wonderful luck of perseverance. Those who have in recent years had a new baby note that the child will have brought you prosperity luck.

Meanwhile the astrological indications of the year are predicting a transformational year. There are no signs of the physical world coming to an end, but the charts do point to a time of great upheavals brought about by the natural disasters of past years and also some rather awesome change; with the world as we know it continuing on a path of transformation started two years ago, and gathering momentum in 2012.

These changes which are political as well as economic, and will impact the lives of many people and change the balance of influence and power in the world. But the good news is that it is also a **year of renewal** - at least the beginnings of good times ahead - of seeing the light at the end of the tunnel.

The Dragon Year always symbolizes an apex of change. It is the celestial creature of Spring, so a year ruled by the Dragon is always a time when the world will experience new beginnings in multiple dimensions of existence.

The 2012 Dragon will see many countries changing directions in terms of allegiances and economic emphasis. New leaders will also emerge and violence could precede or follow upon such change.

Commercially, the world becomes more competitive and demanding. Relationships are edgy and there is an absence of general goodwill. This is due to the preponderance of yearly conflict stars. And there is also the influential *Aggressive Star* hanging over the year's paht chee.

So although natural disasters and severe fallouts caused by weather changes reduce in severity, human conflicts continue to escalate. Tolerance among world leaders is almost nonexistent so we shall hear the rattling of threats and the smell of war. This is compounded by the clashing elements in the year pillar of the Dragon - when Earth clashes with Water - so conflicts do not get resolved. Happily for mankind, this is not a fierce clash. Here, it is Earth stabilizing Water rather than Metal destroying Wood.

It is a year when the presence of the *lap chun* brings the promise of potentially good growth. When growth energy is as strong as it is this year, it brings a good harvest, so symbolically, this is a very encouraging sign.

Also, there is ONE pillar of the paht chee chart that shows a productive relationship between the elements, that of Yang Water producing Yang Wood in the Month pillar. This gives hope of rejuvenation.

The year also sees the heavenly lucky 6 in the center of the feng shui chart, and this brings auspicious luck from above. Engaging the energy of tien or heaven is the key to staying in perfect sync with the year, and is what will unlock good fortune. According to feng shui, this means inviting heavenly and cosmic Deities into the home. This is also a year blessed by the presence of three celestial creatures - the **Dragon**, **Tiger** and **Phoenix** (the presence of the **Rooster** in the year's chart signifies the phoenix) and these bring very welcome powerful and protective energies.

Astrologically therefore, this is a much better year than last year in terms of planting new growth and reaping good harvests. The energies of the Dragon Year are conducive to new ideas and new ways of improving oneself. Investments can be made on healthy foundations and prosperity can be nurtured.

 ENHANCER FOR THE YEAR:
To complete the quartet of celestial protectors it is extremely beneficial if there are tortoises in your home; either you keep live ones, or you at least have the images of these wonderfully auspicious creatures. If you believe in feng shui, you should have tortoises in your homes for they signify not just the protective energy of the Universe; they are also magnificent symbols of longevity.

THE PAHT CHEE CHART OF 2012

This is the Four Pillars chart of the year and reveals not just the general trends of the year but also gives a helicopter view of what can be expected in terms of trends and opportunities. The chart comprises the basket of eight elements that influence the luck of the year.

HOUR	DAY	MONTH	YEAR
HEAVENLY STEM	HEAVENLY STEM	HEAVENLY STEM	HEAVENLY STEM
乙	乙	壬	壬
YIN WOOD	YIN WOOD	YANG WATER	YANG WATER
EARTHLY BRANCH	EARTHLY BRANCH	EARTHLY BRANCH	EARTHLY BRANCH
辛 酉	己 未	甲 寅	戊 辰
METAL ROOSTER	EARTH SHEEP	WOOD TIGER	EARTH DRAGON
HIDDEN HEAVENLY STEMS OF THE YEAR			
-	YIN WOOD YIN FIRE	YANG EARTH YANG FIRE	YIN WATER YIN WOOD
THE YEAR IS DESPERATELY SHORT OF FIRE I.E. INTELLIGENCE & CREATIVITY			

The composition of this basket of elements - Fire, Earth, Metal, Water and Wood - and the frequency of their appearance in the chart - is what shows us what elements are missing, in short supply or in excess. Here is the Paht Chee chart of the year 2012.

We also analyze the chart to determine the stability of the year's energies and go deeper to look for hidden elements that bring additional inputs to the year. The 2012 chart has only four of the five elements, so it is incomplete. There is one element missing. The missing element is FIRE which instantly suggests to anyone who understands the vital importance of balancing the elements that everyone's home will benefit from extra lighting during the coming year. Keeping the home well-lit instantly enhances the energies of any home, bringing a more auspicious foundation for the year.

It is beneficial to install more lights, keep curtains to a minimum and to literally bring the sunshine in. The Fire element in 2012 signifies intelligence and creativity, and there is a shortage of this during the year, so bringing well thought out ideas to any situation improves the success equation.

It is the clever and the wise who will ultimately prevail this year. So curb your impulses and always think things through before making important decisions.

Happily there are **two hidden Fire elements** in the chart and this makes up for the lack of Fire in the main chart. This is a good sign, but hidden Fire can also mean Fire erupting, so there will continue to be calamities associated with hidden Fire.

WOOD ENERGY TOO STRONG IN 2012
Meanwhile, looking deeper into the chart, we see that there is more than enough Wood and Water energy in 2012. In fact, Wood energy is very strong, and could even be too strong. This suggests a degree of **competitiveness that can turn ugly**; excess Wood makes everyone more combative and scheming than usual.

Neither friends nor allies are particularly helpful to each other. The hard-line impulses of the year's energies tend to be pervasive, so for the next twelve months, it is a case of *every man for himself* being the rallying cry. There is also **very serious jostling for power** and rank in many people's lives. Especially amongst leaders, people in charge, and those who supervise others… their motivation will mainly be to outdo and outperform whoever is identified as the challenger. Success this year has to be achieved against this very **competitive scenario**. It plays out on any scale, macro or micro, from the smallest office situation to the global world stage; in the playing fields or in the workplace.

The energy of the working world tends to be antagonistic and hostile, fueled by the presence of the *Aggressive Star*. Words spoken will be louder and more forceful, and especially between those at the top. Amongst patriarchal people, many will tend to be extraterritorial, more assertive and very definitely more uncompromising. This attitude of belligerence will be the main obstacle to harmony this year.

Amongst the four pillars of the chart, you can see that three of them have clashing elements.

In the Year pillar, the heavenly stem of Yang Water clashes with the Earthly branch of Yang Earth. Here the heavenly stem energy is subdued by the earthly branch. The Dragon's earthly influence will be strong.

In the Day pillar, the heavenly stem of **Yin Wood** destroys the Earthly branch of **Yin Earth**. Here, the heavenly stem prevails. The Sheep essence here is subdued by heavenly energy.

In the Hour pillar, the heavenly stem of **Yin Wood** is destroyed by the Earthly branch of **Yin Metal**. We see here the earthly strength of the Rooster.

With 3 out of 4 of the pillars clashing, the year will not be peaceful. Harmony is a hard commodity to come by. But note that in the Month pillar, Yang Water enhances Yang Wood. This is very auspicious as this means there is implied growth energy during the year.

WEALTH LUCK IN 2012 is signified by the element of Earth and with two of these in the main chart as well as one hidden Earth element, there is wealth luck during the year. It should not be difficult for wealth luck to manifest or to get enhanced. What is great is that in the **hidden elements** of this Month pillar, we see the presence of Fire enhancing Earth.

This is a good sign and since it is the Month pillar, it benefits those who undertake wealth-enhancing activities during the months that are favorable for them. So do make an effort to remember your lucky months during the course of the year. Getting your timing right is often the key to making good decisions.

For the Sheep person, the lucky months for engaging in prosperity-enhancing activities are May and July. These two months are when you will benefit most from auspicious luck coming your way, especially May which is a month that has great affinity with your energy this year.

RESOURCE LUCK IN 2012 is represented by the element of Water. There are two direct Water and one hidden Water in the chart and once again, this is a good sign as it means there will be enough resources to keep the year's growth energy stable and strong. In paht chee readings, emphasis is always placed on the stability of good luck manifesting.

This year, Water ensures that the intrinsic Wood energy of the year is kept constantly nourished. The resource availability situation appears good. This also suggests that the price of oil will not be so high as to cause problems to world economic growth. The main danger is that there might be excess Water. Too much Water can create an imbalance, in which case it should be balanced by the presence of Fire energy. The clever balancing of elements in your living space is the key to attracting and sustaining good fortune, so make an effort to increase the presence of Fire energy in your living and working spaces. Use red scatter cushions and red curtains, and enhance your lighting this year!

POWER LUCK IN 2012 is represented by the element of Metal and in the chart there is one occurrence of Metal represented by the earthly branch of the Rooster sign. That there is only a single occurrence of Metal suggests however that power luck in 2012 is not strong; that it is in the Hour pillar means power chi comes more towards the end of the year, and power this year is held by the young person.

The year favors power that is exercised by the younger generation of the family, and more effective when wielded by females.

What is very encouraging is that the **Rooster** and **Dragon** are *Secret Friends* of the Astrological Zodiac. The presence of this auspicious pair of celestial creatures in the year's Paht Chee bodes well for the beginning and end of the year. Their joint presence also subdues to some extent the conflict energy of the year.

Presence of the 3 Celestial Protectors

The Dragon, Phoenix and Tiger appearing together in the chart is also another good indication. These are three of the four celestial guardians of any space. They signify that protector energy is present during the year and to make the energy complete, it is very beneficial in 2012 to invite in the **celestial Tortoise**.

In 2012, all homes benefit from the presence of the **Celestial Tortoise**. Inviting an image of the tortoise into the home is beneficial and timely. Better yet is to start keeping some live tortoises or terrapins. Doing so completes the **powerful quartet** of celestial guardians in your home.

INFLUENCE OF THE PAHT CHEE STARS

In 2012, we see the presence of three powerful stars in the Paht Chee chart. These bring additional dimensions to the year's outlook. They define the attitudes that have a dominant influence on people's tendencies and behavior. The three stars are:

▶ the Star of Aggressive Sword
▶ the Flower of External Romance
▶ the Star of Powerful Mentors

Star of Aggressive Sword

This star suggests a year of intensive aggression. It indicates the strengthening of the underdog's chi energy, so it does point to a continuation of the revolutionary energies started last year. Across the globe, there will be a rise of revolutionary fervor; people revolting against established authority.

At its zenith, the presence of this star suggests the emergence of powerful rebel leaders, or of highly influential opposition to established leaders. It suggests the emergence of people who seize power by fair means or foul. The name of this star is *Yang Ren*, which describes *yang essence sharp blade that inflicts damage.* This is a star that has great potential for either very good or very bad influences to materialize during the year, although generally, the influence tends to be more negative than positive. Unfortunately in the chart of this year, the *Star of Aggressive Sword* is created by the strong Yin Wood of the Day Pillar with the presence of the Tiger in the Month pillar.

Here, note that the Wood element is strong in the chart, making the presence of the Aggressive Sword Star much more negative. It indicates that those emerging as leaders for the underdog in 2012 will end up being heavy-handed and quick-tempered. They are charismatic but will also be strong-willed, arrogant, overbearing and self-centered - all negative traits that spell potential for bloodshed and violence wherever they emerge. This is a real danger for the year!

CURE: If you need protection against being hit by the *Star of Aggressive Sword*, or if you live in a part of the world where revolution has just occurred or where violence prevails, you will need the powerful **Earth Stupa of Protection**. This stupa is filled with powerful *Dharmakaya Relic* mantras and has a protective amulet on its façade which protects against dangers of any kind of violence around you.

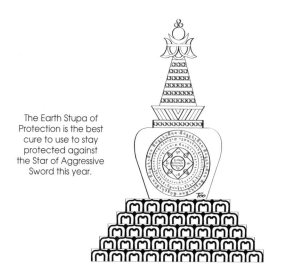

The Earth Stupa of Protection is the best cure to use to stay protected against the Star of Aggressive Sword this year.

Flower of Romance (External)

The *Flower of Romance* is sometimes confused with the *Peach Blossom Star* because it addresses the subject of love. When the flower of romance is present in the Eight Characters chart, it suggests that there is genuine love and caring between husband and wife.

But this is a star that also reveals the **occurrence of extramarital affairs**. The differentiation is made between internal romance and external romance, with the latter implying the occurrence of infidelity.

The *Flower of Romance Star* indicated in this year's chart is that of external romance, so it suggests infidelity within long term love relationships, causing problems and heartaches. Marriages suffer the dangers that this year's flower of romance star poses.

It is thus really helpful to wear or display the safeguards that protect the sanctity of love relationships. In 2012 the external flower of romance is created by the earthly branch Dragon in the Year pillar and the earthly branch Rooster in the Hour pillar.

CURE: To combat this serious affliction, those of you worried about infidelity in your marriage or have cause to suspect your partner of harboring thoughts of infidelity, we suggest you either wear the **amulet which protects against third party interference** (and this is very powerful) OR you can also invite in the image of a Dog & Rabbit to counter the affliction. This subdues the possibility of infidelity causing problems for you. The Dog/Rabbit presence will create a special "cross" with the Dragon/Rooster affliction in the year's chart.

Star of Powerful Mentors

Chinese Astrology makes much of "mentor" luck, and in the old days, having a powerful patron looking after your career path at the Emperor's court was an important success factor. The prospects facing young scholars hoping to rise to powerful positions at the Court of the Emperor was always enhanced with the help of someone influential. In modern times, it is just as excellent to enjoy the luck of being supported by powerful benefactors.

In 2012, the Star of Powerful Mentors emphasizes the importance of Mentor Luck, so those having someone powerful to help them in their career will have the edge.

To attract Mentor Luck, display **Kuan Kung, the God of Advancement and Wealth** in the front part or in the Northwest of the home. The presence of this Taoist Deity attracts the powerful support of a patriarchal figure that will bring good influence to the lives of those about to embark on a career. Kuan Kung also protects against violence that may harm the patriarch!

FLYING STAR NUMBERS OF 2012

The Flying Star chart of 2012 is dominated by the auspicious heavenly star number 6 in the center. This is a strong star. It brings a multi-dimensional manifestation of unexpected good fortune, especially when it gets activated.

Activating any good flying star in any year is part of practicing time dimension feng shui.

There are three effective ways of putting this energy to work for you, all three of which are done with the intention of attracting yang chi into the part of the home which houses the auspicious star number, in this case the number 6 in the center of the home or the center of any room. The three methods of activating yang chi are:

Firstly, create noise...
with a radio or television placed here in the center.

Secondly, create activity...
by having a sitting arrangement here. Human energy is most powerful in activating the *chi*.

Thirdly, create light...

place a bright light in the place where the 6 is located. In 2012, this has a double benefit, as Fire energy represented by light is what brings excellent balancing feng shui.

When energized in any of these three ways, the number 6 will be activated to bring good energies into the home. It is also possible to enhance this star number further by placing powerful **Earth element** energy here in the center of the home. The Earth element magnifies the power of metallic 6, so having **crystal or glass balls** on a coffee table in the center of your living room area would be most auspicious indeed. The best is to have at least a couple of crystal balls that have auspicious images, mantras or sutras lasered on to the crystal. Or to display a large crystal ball that strengthens the Earth element of your Sheep sign.

Remember that crystals are a very effective empowering medium and above all things, crystals bring harmony and a sense of loving kindness into the home. Crystals also empower Earth energy which in 2012 brings prosperity luck.

The feng shui benefits of displaying **six smooth crystal balls** (around 2 to 3 inches in diameter will do, although it is often good to have one super large crystal ball amongst the 6) in the home always brings harmony and enhances loving energies. In 2012, this is one thing that would be extremely beneficial to bear in mind.

> In 2012, it is a good idea to activate the Fire element inside the home, as this element, which represents intelligence and creativity, is missing from the feng shui chart.

Enhancing the home with strengthened Fire will activate the good star numbers of the chart. You can do this by introducing a red crystal ball (preferably lasered with something auspicious or sacred) placed amongst the rest of them on your coffee table. You can also add more light into the heart of your home - consider installing brighter light bulbs or bringing in white lampshades that create pockets of lit-up areas throughout your home.

We have designed an especially auspicious **Hum lampshade** inscribed with the wishfulfilling mantra which is extremely beneficial to place in the center of your living room. Turning on the light each evening will energize the attributes of the *Hum* syllable and also empower the mantra. Also add extra light to the Southwest corner of the home. Adding to the brightness of the Southwest sector of the home strongly enhances the matriarchal energy while subduing the hostile star number 3 which flies there in 2012. This will strengthen the mother energy of the home, which benefits the mother figure of the family and these benefits extend to the entire family.

Note that Southwest is also the Sheep's location and enhancing it with bright lights brings amazing benefits to the Sheep, especially if your bedroom is also located here. The Fire energy of bright lights subdues the number 3 star disturbing you this year. So the more effectively you can light up the Southwest, the more you will benefit.

The Hum lampshade activates the Fire element so-needed in 2012 and also sends blessings in all directions within the home.

FLYING STAR CHART OF 2012

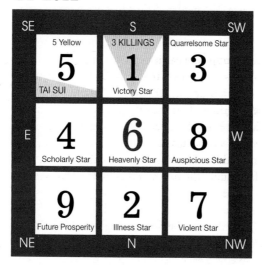

The chart here reveals how the nine numbers of the original Lo Shu square are laid out in the different sectors of the home for 2012. This is probably the best way to understand the feng shui pattern of the year, as it shows how energy congregates within any built-up structure. The nine numbers laid out as shown should be superimposed onto the layout plans of homes and offices in order to understand the luck of sectors, corners and rooms in the home or office.

Every level of the home is affected
by the chart, so it is necessary to
superimpose the chart on every floor
level of your home/office.

Each of the numbers carries energy which can
be auspicious or unlucky. The numbers each have
an intrinsic meaning which reflects luck patterns
congregating in each of the different compass sectors
of the home. Feng shui practitioners are familiar with
all the afflictive and auspicious natures of the nine
numbers; and lineage texts on feng shui offer specific
ways of subduing the bad numbers and enhancing the
lucky numbers.

This is basically how the feng shui of homes can be
updated and improved each year. It is a method that
has not failed, so each year, the updating procedures
to ensure feng shui continues to be good requires the
chart of the year to be analyzed and acted upon.

Enhancing the 6 in the Center

The most important thing to do first is to strengthen
the center number 6, which is auspicious, by
increasing lights in the center and displaying **Earth
element energy** here with **crystal balls** or other
auspicious images made of crystal.

If you can afford them, you can display **crystal images** that have genuine **24 carat gold** embedded within. This is extremely lucky for the everyone within the household and also attracts wealth and prosperity luck for the family.

Strengthening the 1 in the South

The victory star 1 flies to the South, bringing good fortune success luck to bedrooms located here in 2012. So if you sleep in such a room you will enjoy the luck of victory and success.

You can also place the image of a **Horse** here as the Horse brings hidden powers of courage and endurance to the South sector. You can do this even though you are born in the Sheep year. Besides the Horse is your secret friend as well as your *Housemate*. The Sheep and the Horse have enormous affinity with each other so sleeping in the South sector is also beneficial for you.

Displaying the **Banner of Victory** in the South of the living area OR having a **small water feature** here are other excellent ways to cause the **power energy** in the home to manifest. This will be especially beneficial to the young women of the family - i.e. the daughters of the family.

Activating the 8 in the West

All those whose bedrooms are located in the West of their home will benefit from the powerful number 8 star, which flies into this corner in 2012. Here, the auspicious effect of the 8 star is strongly magnified by the *Yi Duo Star* which has also flown here brought by the compass stars of the 24 Mountain directions.

The 8 star also benefits all those whose main entrance into their homes are located in the West sector. You can enhance the foyer area of your home with brighter lighting as Fire enhances the Earth element of the 8 star. You can also place a **red crystal ball with sutra** here or in your West-situated bedroom to activate the power of 8. Also try and keep the door opened as much as possible to let the energy of 8 flow in.

Note that using the Fire element to activate the 8 star also subdues the Metal element of the West. Metal weakens the Earth star 8, so having it subdued will enhance the balance in favor of the 8 star. The advice given here also benefits all those with offices located in the West part of their building.

Those looking for more things to display in the foyer to improve the auspiciousness of their abode can also place the **liu li figure 8** here; or an image of the **Phoenix**. This not only activates the West sector but also the presence of the Rooster in the year's paht chee chart.

Good feng shui is very much about enhancing the energy patterns of the home and placement of the correct symbols in the correct corners of the home does go a very long way towards doing this.

Nurturing the 4 in the East

Contrary to what some believe, the number 4 does not bring negative connotations or bad luck under the flying star system and in fact is the number most often associated with peach blossom or romance.

 MARRIAGE PROSPECTS: Feng shui traditionalists regard the number 4 as the number which enhances the opportunities of marriage within families whose main entrance doors face its location, and for those whose bedrooms are placed where it flies into for the year. In 2012, the number 4 flies to the East.

The element of the East is Wood, which is in harmony with the element of 4, which is also Wood. But the energy of the number 4 star is not strong. This is because it is also affected by the *Star of Reducing Energy* brought by the compass stars of the 24 mountains. As such, it is advisable to strengthen the number 4 star with Water element energy here. Placing a water feature here is one way of doing this. So if your home is facing East, or if your main door is in the East sector of the home, having Water element energy here would be very helpful in activating the positive attributes of the 4 star.

STUDY LUCK: Note that the number 4 is also regarded as the **scholarly star**, bringing luck to all kinds of academic pursuits. If your family comprise children or teenagers still at school or in College, nurturing the number 4 star with a small water feature brings them good fortune luck to their studies, in their examinations and to their applications for admissions into reputable Colleges.

It is however worthwhile noting that the water features used must not be too big, otherwise the number 4 can turn ugly, bringing the affliction of

CHAPTER 1 : DRAGON YEAR 2012

infidelity and sexual scandal. So keep the presence of water here properly balanced.

Magnifying the 9 in the Northeast

This number represents future prosperity. It is also the magnifying number which expands both good and bad. Note that the intrinsic element of 9 is Fire, another reason it is so welcome here in the Northeast. The Fire element enhances the sector's Earth element, strengthening the energy of this part of the house. The Sheep benefits from having a bedroom is here as you then enjoy the benefits that 9 brings, including the luck of future prosperity.

If your door faces Northeast or is located in the Northeast of the home, it will be very beneficial to add lights to this sector at the start of the year. Enhance the lighting of the doorway area of the home both inside and outside. Doing so will magnify the longterm luck prospects of the family.

ENHANCER: The Northeast benefits from there being extra Fire element generated here. So do place extra lights here; better yet, place the **Hum lampshade** or something **bright red in color** here - perhaps red cushions, curtains or a red-dominated art piece.

Subduing the Illness Star 2 in the North

In 2012 the illness star 2 flies to the North, bringing the sickness affliction to all those whose bedrooms are placed in the North of their homes. And if the front door is placed in the North sector, then the effect of this affliction affects everyone living within.

The illness star is an Earth element star, and happily, its flight into the North does not strengthen it, unlike last year when the illness star in the South brought a great deal of sickness to many people.

Nevertheless, it is a good idea to subdue this affliction as it is never pleasant getting sick or succumbing to the fever bug, the coughing bug or the flu bug. Worse, the illness star weakens the resistance of all those whose life force or chi energy is not strong.

The Sheep's Life Force however is not weak so if your bedroom is here just place the **wu lou** in your bedroom and be extra careful in September - that is when you are hurt by the illness star.

Suppressing Yellow Star 5 in the Southeast

Those familiar with feng shui afflictions know how awful the yellow star 5 can be. This star number brings a whole series of bad news, illness, obstacles to success and all kinds of depressing feelings. It creates an aura of despondency and unhappiness and causes moods and attitudes to just go haywire.

It rarely surprises us when those affected by the 5 Yellow start being more sensitive than usual to imagined slights, or become more prone to finding faults with others. In 2012, this affliction affects those whose bedrooms or main doors are situated in or facing the Southeast direction.

CURE FOR THE FIVE YELLOW: A good cure continues to be the five element pagoda with the gem wishfulfilling tree. The pagoda with the tree of life which we brought out last year continues to be a powerful remedy for this afflictive star. In 2012 however, it is very beneficial to add the powerful seed syllables associated with purifying Fire energy, as this has the added advantage of engaging the spiritually powerful cures associated with these symbols.

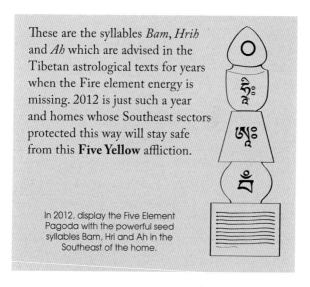

These are the syllables *Bam*, *Hrih* and *Ah* which are advised in the Tibetan astrological texts for years when the Fire element energy is missing. 2012 is just such a year and homes whose Southeast sectors protected this way will stay safe from this **Five Yellow** affliction.

In 2012, display the Five Element Pagoda with the powerful seed syllables Bam, Hri and Ah in the Southeast of the home.

Suppressing the Star 7 in the Northwest

The 7 star wreaked some real havoc last year, bringing violence, death and suffering to many countries in the Middle East, as well as into households whose central sector were somehow not protected against this afflictive number.

This year, the number 7 flies to the Northwest, directly affecting the luck and prospects of the patriarch of households. This usually refers to the man of the family and to the leaders of countries and companies.

It brings danger of robbery and violence to those living in this part of the home; and in the office, if your desk is located here, chances are you could feel the negativity of being betrayed and let down.

 CURE: The best cure for the 7 star in the Northwest for this year 2012 is Water energy. The presence of water near a **Blue Elephant** and a **Blue Rhino** would be extremely auspicious and this is because the metal element of the Northwest strengthens the 7 star. Water is needed to weaken the Metal energy.

Subduing the Star 3 in the Southwest

In 2012 the hostile quarrelsome star number 3 flies into the location of the matriarch i.e. the Southwest. This suggests that angry mood swings afflict the mother energy of homes affecting the harmony of families and the safety of marriages.

Those whose bedrooms are located in the Southwest will be especially influenced by this star number and they should make every effort to suppress it with strong fire energy. The number 3 star is a Wood element star and it is best dealt with using Fire energy.

This star number attracts the bad luck of having to cope with problems arising from the law. Court cases, litigation & quarrelsome energy will make life extremely difficult and aggravating for you. All of this affects the Sheep, so you should be very mindful of the cures that can subdue this affliction.

If your door faces the Southwest, it is best to try using another door and you should definitely try to increase lighting in this part of the house to suppress the 3 star.

CURE FOR THE #3 STAR:
In 2012, the best cure for the number 3 star would be the **Magic Diagram Red Sword Mirror** which can suppress all hostile energy brought by other people's jealous intentions. This is a powerful feng shui implements and are very effective for slicing through the negative intentions of others aimed at you. Placed in the **Southwest,** this strengthens the Chi Essence of the Mother figure in households.

THE STARS OF
THE 24 MOUNTAINS

We also examine a third set of data which influence
what the year brings to each of the twelve animal
signs. These are the **compass fortune stars** of the 24
Mountains, which change each year. Their influence
on the luck profile of animal signs is meaningful,
and working to subdue their negative influences or
enhance their positive ones is an excellent way of
improving one's fortunes for the year.

**Different lucky and unlucky
fortune stars fly into each of the
24 compass sectors each year,
bringing energies that either
improve or decrease the energy of
the 12 animal signs.**

There are 108 different fortune stars, but only a handful
fly into each of the 24 Mountain directions in any year.
These bring auspicious or harmful influences, which
vary in strength and type each year. The stars for 2012
are not as full of promise as they were last year.

This year we see a big number of **conflict stars**
suggesting that the signs affected are in conflict with
the year. Conflict signs are not auspicious; nor do they

24 MOUNTAINS CHART OF 2012

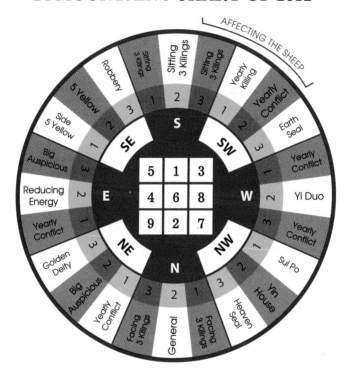

The 24 Mountains Compass brings the Sheep the Yearly Killing, Yearly Conflict and sitting Three Killings star, which cause conflicts in relationship and other aggravations. These afflictions need to be subdued with proper cures for Sheep to get the best out of the year.

bring anything but disharmony and obstacles, so those affected should strive to either use amulet or gem therapy to counter the potential conflict brought by the compass fortune stars.

> **Gem therapy** uses the power of planetary influences and usually calls on activating one's favorable planets based on each animal sign's lucky days of birth - which can be their *Day of Excellence* or their *Day of Vitality*.

Animal signs that are negatively affected by the stars of the 24 mountains should wear the "gemstone" that activates the planet that strengthens their *Day of Vitality*, and if possible, also their *Day of Excellence*.

So it is useful to know the gemstone to wear that will help you subdue 24 mountain star afflictions such as conflict stars, that are stationed at or near your Zodiac sign location.

Each day of the week is ruled by one of the seven powerful planets, which can be activated by wearing the gemstone associated with the planet.

The SUN enhances Sundays and the gemstone which strengthens the energy of the Sun are all the red colored stones - rubies, rubellites and red tourmalines.

☾ The **MOON** strengthens the energy of Mondays and gemstones associated with the Moon are light colored pearls (preferably white) and the Moonstone. Crystals are also good for nurturing Moon energy to strengthen Mondays.

♂ The planet **MARS** nurtures the energy of Tuesdays and Mars is associated with red colored stones, although it is coral rather than any of the beryls or crystal stones that strengthens Mars.

☿ The planet **MERCURY** enhances Wednesdays and gemstones associated with this planet are all the green stones, which include jade, emeralds, as well as green tourmalines.

♃ The planet **JUPITER** enhances Thursdays and gemstones associated with this planet are all the yellow colored stones, the best of which are yellow diamonds and sapphires, although citrines are also excellent for pacifying Jupiter.

♀ The planet **VENUS** rules Friday and the gemstones associated with this planet are all the light blue colored stones such as aquamarines and blue topazes.

♄ **The planet SATURN** rules Saturdays and the gemstones associated with this planet are the dark blue sapphires.

Unfortunately for the Sheep, you are afflicted by the *Star of Yearly Killing* so it is beneficial and even necessary to enhance your *Day of Vitality* thus improving your energy synchronizations with that of the year. Strengthening your vitality will enhance your luck for the year and help reduce the severity of the yearly killing affliction.

Note that for the Sheep, your personal lucky *Day of Vitality* is **Wednesday** which is ruled by the planet Mercury, so wearing green stones such as Jade or Emeralds will boost your vitality and your inner strength. Your *Day of Excellence* is **Friday** which is ruled by Venus, so wearing light blue aquamarines is most beneficial.

Meanwhile also note that you should refrain from wearing yellow stones as these will activate the planet Jupiter. Doing so brings obstacles into your life. This is because Thursday is your Day of Obstacles.

Beneficial Signs

Two directions benefit from the 24 mountains, and these are Southwest 3 and Northwest 3, both of which directions enjoy the good fortune of receiving the **Earth and Heaven Seals** respectively.

The good thing about these seals is that if only just one member or resident of a household enjoys the support of the heaven or earth seal, based on their animal sign - in this case the **Monkey** and the **Boar** respectively - it benefits the whole household.

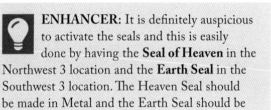

ENHANCER: It is definitely auspicious to activate the seals and this is easily done by having the **Seal of Heaven** in the Northwest 3 location and the **Earth Seal** in the Southwest 3 location. The Heaven Seal should be made in Metal and the Earth Seal should be made in crystal.

This year's 24 Mountains energy pattern manifests only two stars of *Big Auspicious* and these occur in the East 3 location and the Northeast 2 location. If your bedroom is located in either of these two locations, you are sure to benefit from something big coming your way.

The Affliction Stars Around the Sheep

The Sheep is sitting directly on the *Yearly Killing Star* in 2012 and this means you need to be watchful over your temper. Make sure you do not allow anger energy to overcome you as it can get ugly, especially since next to you is the star of 3 killings.

These "killing" stars in feng shui terms means loss of some kind and it is a good idea to place the **three celestial guardians** in these locations as a safeguard. It is definitely advisable to wear at least one protective amulet as protection against getting hit by bad energy.

On your other side meanwhile is the *Star of Yearly Conflict* - so there are really not one but several indications of violence and conflict vibrations surrounding the Sheep. You would be well advised to be extra careful about your safety this year!

These are serious afflictions and it would be extremely helpful for you to invoke the protection of your Guardian Deity. This engages the third dimension to your luck - which is the empowerment of the cosmic auras around you. Place images of the **three celestial guardians** and stay mindful of the hostility minefields the year. Be extra careful during the months of

August and **October** when the negative afflictions lined up against you double in strength.

Keeping Track of Your Good Months

Every year we emphasize the huge importance of timing in the way you manage your year and in how you can ensure that the important decisions you make as well as the actions you take through the course of the year are done at times when your luck is riding high.

As such, tracking the astrological flight of monthly stars is important, as this is what lets you see what months bring good energy and what months are better for you to avoid making important decisions or taking important action.

In these books we examine the way the monthly stars affect each of the 12 signs to include detailed analysis of your luck month by month. This gives you a blueprint for when to lie low and when to strike out, take risks and start projects dear to you.

These monthly analyses highlight timely warnings that enable you to avoid accidents, avoid meeting up with bad people, getting burgled or succumbing to health risks. Good and bad months for travel are likewise highlighted.

> Monthly updates analyze each month's Lo Shu numbers, element, trigram and paht chee luck pillars. These pinpoint your lucky and unlucky months and give valuable pointers on how to navigate safely and successfully through the year.

Aggravating obstacles can be avoided; whatever misfortune vibes that lie ahead can be circumnavigated. You can then take timely precautions either by installing remedies or by making sure you wear the necessary protection to avoid these obstacles altogether.

The monthly updates are an important component of these books as recommendations are detailed and clear cut. Through the years we have received hundreds of thank you letters from readers telling us how they successfully followed our books and reduced the impact of accidents, burglaries and illnesses.

Improving Luck Using Compass Directions

In 2012, the use of correct facing and sitting directions - i.e. activating your personalized lucky directions - will help you stay protected against inadvertently getting hit by unlucky or disastrous transformational energies. So we have devoted a larger section this year on helping you to get your facing directions right. These are customized to assist all Sheep-born to finetune their lucky and unlucky Kua directions.

Compass Direction Feng Shui

This is one of the more effective ways of making sure the energies around you help rather than hinder you, no matter what you may be engaging in through the year. The energies of the 2012 Dragon Year are strong and particularly compelling, with good and bad luck making a big impact on people's lives.

The Dragon's powerful energy needs to be controlled and managed. It is a minefield of a year in terms of belligerence and violence, anger and antagonism; these hostile vibes are strongly prevalent. It is a year when the three celestials - **Dragon, Tiger and Phoenix** desperately need the calming effect of the **celestial cosmic Tortoise**. The **aura of the Tortoise** is legendary and having its presence can be very beneficial. But getting your directions right while sleeping, working, eating, talking and so forth will also go a long way towards safeguarding your luck this year.

Do take this advice seriously. It is really no fun being hit by bad energy; this will happen if you inadvertently face a direction that is out of sync with your sign especially when doing something important or when talking to someone important. The key is to activate directions that are lucky for you and lucky this year as well.

Spiritual Feng Shui

Finally, as something new, we are including in this year's books a whole chapter on powerful cosmic feng shui, that suggest a customized amulet that is suitable for the Sheep sign to wear or display as well as the offering incense ritual to practice.

There are amulets and rituals that ward off bad luck, protect against being obstructed in your business and your career, as well as to attract specific kinds of good fortune for those building a new house, having a baby, starting a new venture, getting married, embarking on a long journey or wanting and needing cosmic assistance on a specific project.

Amulets may be worn on special chakra points of the body or displayed in certain corners of frequently used rooms. This is part of the Third Dimension of feng shui, a dimension that makes the practice of feng shui much more complete.

Different animal signs benefit from different kinds of amulets, and wearing those that are best for your sign will help you to stay on top of the elements affecting you during the year.

In astrology, keeping the elements balanced is the key to unlocking good fortune, but when this is helped along by **cosmic Sanskrit symbols** and powerful mantras, the effect becomes incredibly potent as it taps directly into the cosmic power of spiritual feng shui.

By bringing in the third dimension into our luck equation, we will also be enhancing the feng shui of our living spaces. Space is enhanced with environmental feng shui methods through the optimum placement of furniture and auspicious objects.

Good space feng shui also means good design of layout and flow of chi. It takes note of compass directions on a personalized basis and uses other methods to identify lucky and unlucky sectors. Broadly speaking, it takes care of the Earth aspect in the trinity of luck.

Time dimension feng shui addresses energy pattern changes over time and is founded on the premise that energy is never static but is constantly changing. This means good feng shui requires regular updating by taking into account overlapping cycles of time; annually, monthly, daily, hourly and even in larger time frames that last 20 years and 60 years.

It takes 180 years to complete a full nine period cycle of 20 years. These books address the annual and monthly cycles of change that affect everyone differently. These cycles are viewed within the larger context of the Period of 8 cycle, which deals with the heavenly cosmic forces within the trinity of luck.

Using, wearing and displaying amulets is part of the spiritual third dimension, which focuses on energies generated by mankind. In concert with cosmic forces, the strength of amulets is derived from the individual's own yang chi, and this is created by the mind's connections to the cosmos.

Self energy in its purest form is the most powerful kind of energy. This is *Mankind Chi* which combines with heaven and earth to create the trinity of luck. The empowered self generates copious amounts of positive spiritual chi and this can be directed into amulets to empower them.

When consecrated (i.e. energized) by Masters who possess highly concentrated energies through their superior practices, these amulets take on great potency. To possess concentrated spiritual power requires years of practice; there are methods - both gross and subtle - that can be learnt which are collectively part of the inner feng shui traditions of feng shui.

In the old days, Masters of the old school were great adepts at these kinds of transcendental practice and they often made special amulets with their knowledge, to give to those who came to them for help. Some of these amulets were made according to the animal sign of birth of those asking for them.

These Masters were devotees of Taoist or Buddhist spiritual Deities; many increased their own cosmic powers through regular daily meditations, reciting powerful mantras and sutras and using secret rituals to remove obstacles.

In the practice of astrological traditions, the **Tibetan practitioners of cosmic magic** generally invoke powerful Buddhist Deities who awaken within these individuals their own inner forces, sometimes bringing them to pretty high levels of siddhic accomplishments.

This aspect of feng shui or luck invocation has only rarely been leaked out into the world. Many of the most effective methods and rituals, sutras and magical mantras are still secret, or have not yet been translated. Masters familiar with these practices reveal their secrets only to a favored few.

A few of these secrets have made their way to us, and one discovery we have made are the secrets related to creating and consecrating amulets and filling them with powerful mantras according to the animal sign of birth. For the Sheep, we have included here an amulet which will benefit you just by carrying this book near you. We have also discovered that powerful incense rituals using specially formulated aromas and offered to the local cosmic protectors can be used to overcome life and success obstacles.

We have since found the incense formulations and ingredients that work best at clearing obstacles and appeasing local spirits and made them into ready to use incense pellets. You can buy them in packets and learn the special incantations that empower them.

For the Sheep, we recommend to use incense to clear bad luck afflictions during the months of February, June, August, October and November this year.

The Sheep has several irksome months to cope with and it is beneficial to engage the help of the landlords of your living space. Appeasing them with aromatic incense engages their assistanc,e which brings you invisible protection against conflict and killing energies. These are weaknesses in your year's chart and they can definitely be appeased with the incense offering rituals.

Incense rituals can remove obstacles and make your path to success smoother and a lot less aggravating.

Amulet for the Sheep-born. Carrying this amulet near you at all times
will keep you safe from harmful energies through the year.

Chapter Two

THE SHEEP IN 2012
Luck Prospects &
Energy Strength

- Metal Sheep – 21 & 81 years
- Water Sheep – 69 years
- Wood Sheep – 57 years
- Fire Sheep – 45 years
- Earth Sheep – 33 years

Outlook for the Sheep In 2012

With your life force and your chi essence improving also comes a very significant increase & improvement in your Success luck. In 2012, all those born in the Sheep year will enjoy significant attainments. Projects get completed and all that you are striving to achieve will get actualized. There will be fewer obstacles blocking your way so that those engaged in competitive pursuits will experience the attainment factor easily.

Those of you in a career or professional situation will find that the year can also bring meaningful recognition and those of you up for upward promotion will have something to smile about as well. Success luck is an enormously precious commodity, especially in this particular Year of the Dragon when many others have to overcome the afflictions of cosmic obstacles.

In terms of Finance Luck, all Sheep (except the 45 year old Fire Sheep) also enjoy improved financials. There is greater stability in your economic situation with the 57 year old Wood Sheep having a financial bonanza year.

The Wood element in the heavenly stem of your year of birth brings you wealth luck from the heavens, so it will be something unexpected and from a source that could prove surprising.

Many of you will also enjoy good health luck this year, except for the 33 year old Earth Sheep who will be focusing too intensively on work and on building their career profiles. So apart from this particular Sheep, all others can have a perfectly good time indulging yourself in physical type activities. It is also a year when travelling brings much needed relaxation time.

The main anxiety facing the Sheep's luck this year is the problem of anger management. While for many of you, 2012 can turn out to be a great year of growth and expansion, there is also the possibility that hot tempers and impatience could well spoil everything for you. There is no bigger enemy than the enemy of the angry self, so do make a very special effort to keep hostility energy at bay. Consciously work at staying patient; keep your cool and try hard not to respond with anger in any situation whatsoever.

It is just NOT worth it compromising all the good energy coming your way by giving in to anger. Even when others annoy or aggravate you better not to respond at all. Or when someone makes you lose face or try to humiliate you, it is better to smile off these attempts. Tell yourself it is only the number 3 feng shui affliction that is making you angry or is causing others to make you angry. Thinking this way is sure to help you count from one to ten and then bring a smile to your face.

For all Sheep-born, treat this year as one of building and growing. Many of you are helped in your efforts by lucky elements that bring you strength and courage. The feng shui flying stars are not very helpful but this Dragon Year is when the greater Universe is bringing transformational energies. Hence if at times you feel uncertain, it is understandable because your inner chi strength is not as strong as it can be. Strengthen this with greater mind power. Use your own will power to enhance your inner strength - then only can you feel empowered to confidently grab at the good fortune elements that are bringing you cosmic opportunities for growth and success.

The luck of the five kinds of Sheep based on the element interactions of their heavenly stems with those of year are indicated as follows. This reflects the Sheep's overall luck for the year:

Water Sheep – A very good year for you.
Wood Sheep – Superb year for wealth creation.
Fire Sheep – Victory, but money luck lacking.
Earth Sheep - Success luck but watch health.
Metal Sheep – Strong recognition luck.

OUTLOOK FOR
THE SHEEP IN 2012

The Sheep is better off digging its heels in this year and focusing on what it wants to achieve. Outstanding success luck brings you attainment vibes that can bring quite spectacular achievements to your efforts. There is huge recognition luck as well, so this is a year when effort and industry pays off really well.

Do not rely on your instincts alone. Instead, think things through before deciding on your course of action. Strategize carefully when it comes to taking action and do not make big decisions based purely on feelings.

In this Year of the Dragon, let your head rule your heart. This is not a year to listen to your inner voice simply because your inner voice is just not that reliable this year. Your chi strength is not at all strong and relying on it can bring more problems rather than solutions.

But you can be assured that for most of you at least, the year's element energies sync well with yours, so you can be as courageous and as confident as you want to be - just always think before jumping into any commitment or risky venture. But you must be prepared for hard work and great effort. There are also conflict energies and problematic hurdles through the year. It is not all plain sailing, so irrespective of where you work and what you do, whether you are a business person or working for someone or for some company, this is a year when you will need to grit your teeth and power through some challenging moments.

Take note that you must at all times be aware of the greater cosmic energies that bring a scenario of change to the year and this affects you both directly and indirectly.

There are major afflictive stars this year that cause even the best laid plans to go awry, so if anything happens to force you to change directions, make new plans and steer in new directions. You must just grin and bear it and then dig in to pursue new directions.

In 2012, the Sheep is influenced by the Three Killings, sitting on the Yearly Killing Star, as well as having the Yearly Conflict Star on its left... These troublesome stars must be dealt with and subdued.

First you need to overcome the *Star of Three Killings*, then the *Star of Yearly Killing* and finally the *Star of Yearly Conflict*. These are all unfriendly stars but they can be dealt with and they can be neutralized. All you need is the knowledge of the remedies and the will to subdue them.

 CURE 1: You can display any of the three celestial guardians - **the Chi Lin, the Fu Dog and the Pi Yao** or all three together. Place them in the South3 and Southwest 1 locations. i.e. where the Sheep resides and right next to it on the Sheep's right. This will keep the three killings star subdued. This will also subdue the *Yearly Killing Star*.

By having these three celestial guardians in this part of the house will ensure protection against hindrances brought by wandering cosmic negatives. These subdue anything that might cause you illness, depression or loss of confidence. These celestials also give you a big boost of courage so do invite them into your home.

As for the *Yearly Conflict Star* in the Southwest 2 location, this reflects the number hostile star of misunderstanding brought by feng shui winds in the flying star chart. So here we see conflict energy doubled and it is really vital then to suppress all hostility vibes otherwise you could get really distracted and made distraught by inconvenient misunderstandings and worse yet, a battle royal in the courts.

Even if it is not initiated by, others could charge you on legal matters forcing you to have days of hostility in the courtroom. This is unfortunately what the number 3 star brings each time it enters into your sector on the astrology wheel.

> **CURE 2:** The second important cure you will need to put into place in the Southwest of your home is something that depicts the Fire energy. This element is missing from the year's basket of elements, so Fire energy brings a double benefit. It is both an enhancer and a cure. In the Southwest sector, it has both of these benefits. The Fire will subdue all conflict energy here while also ensuring a balanced year.

The solution is for the Sheep to place something red in its own Southwest sector. This creates Fire energy which strengthens this earth corner. Display the **red crystal ball** with the heart sutra OR place the **Hum lampshade** here in your home location. The all powerful Hum syllable, kept activated by the light of the lampshade is both auspicious and protective.

Keep the lampshade turned on every day and if you can, add some other crystal globes under the lamp shade as this will bring great harmony into your life and your home. Crystal balls have enormous capacity to absorb conflict vibes especially when there is a light activating them. This should take care of the *Yearly Conflict Star* on the left of your home location in the compass wheel of the year. The best is always to display crystal globes that have auspicious symbols such as ingots or gold embedded within them.

Do make an effort to keep all the other lights in your Southwest 1 location of the house or living room a little brighter than usual as this adds to the store of Fire element energy that then directly benefits the Sheep living within the home.

The Sheep is definitely enjoying a better year in 2012 than in the previous year, and this spills over into your personal and love life as well. Those who are married might see a "happiness occasion" i.e. maybe a new baby or a marriage of one of your children. Should there indeed be such a *hei* occasion in your household, welcome it as a very good sign.

You can also create such an occasion by throwing an evening of festivity celebrating a birthday of an older person. As for relationship luck, note that your friends will see you as something of a workaholic this year; in 2012, many of you will also have a very sociable year.

OUTLOOK FOR THE LADY SHEEP IN 2012

The Sheep lady is actually a lot tougher than her appearance suggests and even if she may be lacking in courage inside, her calm demeanor will not allow outsiders to see or even feel her nervousness. There is a great deal of steel within the Sheep woman, and it is this inner courage that keeps her plodding along against sometimes great odds. In 2012, many of you will need to call on this inner strength even though the charts suggest a lacking of inner chi strength. This is because there is quite a fair bit of conflict energy that calls for your attention and your wisdom.

BIRTH YEAR	TYPE OF SHEEP LADY	LO SHU NO.	AGE	LUCK OUTLOOK IN 2012
1943	Water Sheep Lady	3	69	Overall a very good year
1955	Wood Sheep Lady	9	57	Excellent money & success luck
1967	Fire Sheep Lady	6	45	Good success but low on finances
1979	Earth Sheep Lady	3	33	Money & attainments come your way
1991	Metal Sheep Girl	9	21	Good success brings attainments

Outwardly the Sheep lady may appear vulnerable, and indeed, many of you take pride in appearing simply too feminine to be strong. Nothing could be further from the truth however, and this is a good thing.

Amongst the signs of the Zodiac, the Sheep lady is usually described as the most clever of all the women in an Emperor's harem, being superlatively charming as far as the opposite sex is concerned. Men fall for her and find her irresistible as she is usually able to maintain interest long after any casual first meeting.

There is something about her which inspires love and faithfulness. This is probably due to her genuine thoughtfulness and kindness towards others.

The Sheep woman is usually soft spoken, rarely raising her voice, and almost never confrontational, so mixing with her is usually a relaxing experience. Unfortunately for her, and for those around her this year, she will tend to be a lot more impatient and a lot less patient in her interactions with others. This comes from the hostile vibes afflicting her persona... by the feng shui winds of the year.

So this year she will be more nitpicking, more easily finding fault and also more demanding of her spouse and children. This does not mean she will be too impossibly difficult, but it does mean that she is harder to please. She will seem more critical than before, so those close to her must understand that her inner core being has not changed. It is only the year's energies getting the better of her, causing aggravation vibes to get the better of her.

The luckiest Sheep lady in 2012 is the **57 year old Wood Sheep** whose luck appears to be at a very high level indeed. Perhaps it is her age, or perhaps it is the Wood element in her heavenly stem that gives her amazing will power and drive to actualize the wonderfully strong Finance and Success Luck in her chart. But the **33 year old Earth Sheep** is not far behind in the success and financial stakes either. Both these Sheep women can look ahead to a pretty good and meaningful year. For the **45 year old Fire Sheep** however, there must be extra care placed on your finances. You could see some kind of loss situation this year.

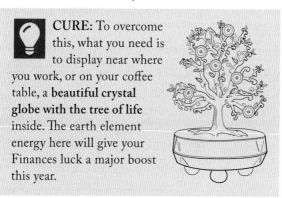

CURE: To overcome this, what you need is to display near where you work, or on your coffee table, **a beautiful crystal globe with the tree of life** inside. The earth element energy here will give your Finances luck a major boost this year.

For the **21 year old Metal Sheep,** the year's energies are focused on career prospects and the good news for you this year is that you will indeed land a good job, one that will bring out the best within you.

OUTLOOK FOR THE GENTLEMAN SHEEP IN 2012

BIRTH YEAR	TYPE OF SHEEP MAN	LO SHU NO.	AGE	LUCK OUTLOOK IN 2012
1943	Water Sheep Man	3	69	An excellent year brings happiness
1955	Wood Sheep Man	9	57	Great money & success
1967	Fire Sheep Man	6	45	Low on funds but very successful
1979	Earth Sheep Man	3	33	A very fulfilling year with success luck
1991	Metal Sheep Boy	9	21	Embarking on a great career path

The Sheep gentleman is as steely and has as much inner strength as his female counterpart, although it is unlikely he will let any of this show through his outward reserve. He is naturally a shy person and is as soft spoken as the female of his sign. But the male Sheep is incredibly charming and very attractive indeed to the opposite sex.

He has an easy charm that makes him very successful with the ladies. Many will describe the Sheep gentleman as attractive and beguiling, possessed of the gift of the gab. But he does not like too many people around him, preferring small intimate groups to big public type gatherings. His tongue is persuasive and diplomatic, so people automatically turn to him whenever the power of speech is required to achieve something. But this may not be very much in evidence in 2012 when conflict vibes cause his tongue to be a little bit more caustic and his attitude a little more hostile than reflects his true nature.

The Sheep guy does not run away in the face of hostile behavior shown towards him but will stand his ground, and this is when the steel within him shows through. He is not necessarily a born leader, being reluctant to lead a large group of people, but he will have nerves of steel to make tough decisions and to see through severe obstacles when it is needed.

He is great also at being highly persuasive in a one on one situation. Intrigues and politics are his *forte*. He does not work the cocktail party circuits smoothly as some others but in the safe confines of private rooms the Sheep gentleman comes into his own. This is how he will operate most successfully in 2012, out of the prying eyes of others; he will forge links, make strategic alliances and close big deals that will reap him BIG rewards.

> The Sheep guy is not confrontational by nature and in fact goes out of his way to avoid direct conflicts. He prefers to suffer in silence but he has a long memory and stores whatever is done for or against him inside his big storehouse of a memory bank. Though he may not be vengeful, he knows how to get his own back without appearing to do so.

Sheep gentlemen tend to get luckier with age. He loves the luxury lifestyle but he is never overtly ambitious; no matter how rich or wealthy he eventually becomes he will seem to take it all in his stride.

Neither his manner nor his expressions or his body language will give much away. In 2012, the Sheep gentleman operates at a handicap as he faces a range of conflict stars and hostile energy. But in the midst of all these obstacles he will prevail.

ENERGY STRENGTH ANALYSIS OF SHEEP LUCK 2012

This section focuses on the element luck analyses of the Sheep in 2012. These reveal five kinds of luck in the Sheep horoscope and are charted according to how the Sheep's ruling luck elements in the year of birth interacts with the elements of the year 2012, thus offering indications of strength or weakness in the horoscope for the year.

Check the five tables here for your five luck categories of luck in 2012. The significance of the luck indications is explained as follows:

First, Your Life Force...

This highlights the hidden dangers to your life. Danger to one's life manifests suddenly and with little warning. In the past two years, clashing elements in the paht chee chart brought raging wildfires, tsunamis, floods, earthquakes and other natural disasters that wreaked havoc and destruction.

Last year, this was compounded by the feng shui chart which brought the violent star 7 to the centre, so we saw raw human anger overflow into revolution that brought danger into the lives of millions of people. Many of these uprisings and disasters happened without warning. Staying safe against being caught unawares is an important aspect of horoscope readings.

For all those born in Sheep years, your Life Force luck shows a healthy O, a single O for 2012 and this means that your Life Force is reasonably strong, and the year should be reasonably safe for you.

There is no big need to worry despite turbulence of the world's energies and the instability of natural forces. But wearing protective amulets is worthwhile doing just to keep and stay safe.

Second, Your Health Luck...

This is the luck of your health condition during the year and it indicates how strongly you can avoid illness bugs. For the Sheep, note that the feng shui chart brings the hostile 3 which brings mental rather than physical ailments.

Nevertheless, it is important to take note of health issues when this luck category indicates a **XX**, as with the **33 year old Earth Sheep**. Only this Sheep has the **XX** against the health luck, so you will need to be careful. Note that when the luck indication is a double cross **XX**, it means that 2012 can bring ailments and vulnerability to health issues; and these will cause obstacles to work schedules. Plans get blocked and opportunities get missed. Poor health luck means you can get food poisoning easily, and you catch wind borne diseases.

It is advisable for the **33 year old Earth Sheep** to use a cure against illness. This is either the **wu lou** or the vase with healing nectar. All the other Sheep have varying health luck ranging from a single **O** to a double **OO** and also an **OX** so for the others, health luck appears good and relatively strong.

Third, Your Finance Luck...

This reveals if you will enjoy financial stability during the year. It is also an indication of whether you can do better than the previous year. The **57 year old Wood Sheep** is showing a triple OOO and this means some very substantial gain of new wealth is coming towards you. The other Sheep having great good fortune in this aspect of their luck is the **33 year old Earth Sheep** who enjoys the luck of two circles i.e. OO. Viewed against the rest of the chart, you enjoy great allround luck as well.

A single circle – **O** – means the year does not bring much change to your finances and you will enjoy a stable situation. There are few surprises to make you worry. This will be the case for the **69 year old Water Sheep**.

An indication of crosses is a negative reading and the more crosses there are the greater the instability of your financial situation. Only one Sheep i.e. the **45 year old Fire Sheep** has a showing of **XX**.

One of the best ways of enhancing wealth luck is to invoke the presence of the Wealth Buddhas; by wearing the Yellow Dzambhala holding a Rat spewing forth jewels or the White Dzambhala sitting on a Dragon.

Wearing these images – as a watch with their mantras perpetually moving is one of the best methods of activating wealth luck and also excellent for the Dragon Year. Or you can also display these Wealth Dzambhalas on a crystal globe. This also activates the wealth element of the year which is Earth.

Fourth, Your Success Luck...

This highlights your attainment luck for the year whether it be success in your professional work or in your studies. Circles are strong indications of success while **XX**s are negative indications suggesting obstacles.

The luck indication for all of you born in Sheep years enjoy a double OO indication and this means you will enjoy a very stable year when it comes to gaining success in all that you do.

Some of you could well enjoy promotions and good recognition luck because of the excellent showing in the feng shui chart. A **OO** indication is usually considered a very strong indication.

Fifth, Your Spirit Essence...

This indicator of chi essence luck reveals insights into your inner resilience and spiritual strength. When strong, it shows you are resistant to spiritual afflictions and can more easily overcome the lack of other categories of luck. Low Spirit Essence is indicated by crosses, and this instantly tells you to be careful and to protect yourself with powerful mantra amulets. The Sheep has a single **X** against its Chi Essence luck and this means that your inner spirit is relatively weak.

To compensate for your weak chi essence you can always wear the **powerful protective seed syllables** touching you and on your body. These can be worn as rings or as pendants touching your heart chakra. Or you might want to consider wearing **protective amulets** specially formulated to bring cosmic protection from spirit harm and bad luck.

To counter low Spirit Essence, wear the seed syllable Hum or Bhrum as a pendant or ring. This provides protection against spirit harm.

WATER SHEEP
69 YEARS OLD

TYPE OF LUCK	ELEMENT AT BIRTH	ELEMENT IN 2012	LUCK RATING
LIFE FORCE	EARTH	EARTH	O
HEALTH LUCK	WOOD	WATER	OOO
FINANCE LUCK	WATER	WATER	O
SUCCESS LUCK	FIRE	WOOD	OOO
SPIRIT ESSENCE	FIRE	FIRE	X

WOOD SHEEP
57 YEARS OLD

TYPE OF LUCK	ELEMENT AT BIRTH	ELEMENT IN 2012	LUCK RATING
LIFE FORCE	EARTH	EARTH	O
HEALTH LUCK	METAL	WATER	OX
FINANCE LUCK	WOOD	WATER	OOO
SUCCESS LUCK	FIRE	WOOD	OOO
SPIRIT ESSENCE	FIRE	FIRE	X

FIRE SHEEP
45 YEARS OLD

TYPE OF LUCK	ELEMENT AT BIRTH	ELEMENT IN 2012	LUCK RATING
LIFE FORCE	EARTH	EARTH	O
HEALTH LUCK	WATER	WATER	O
FINANCE LUCK	FIRE	WATER	XX
SUCCESS LUCK	FIRE	WOOD	OOO
SPIRIT ESSENCE	FIRE	FIRE	X

EARTH SHEEP
33 YEARS OLD

TYPE OF LUCK	ELEMENT AT BIRTH	ELEMENT IN 2012	LUCK RATING
LIFE FORCE	EARTH	EARTH	O
HEALTH LUCK	FIRE	WATER	XX
FINANCE LUCK	EARTH	WATER	OO
SUCCESS LUCK	FIRE	WOOD	OOO
SPIRIT ESSENCE	FIRE	FIRE	X

METAL SHEEP
21 YEARS OLD

TYPE OF LUCK	ELEMENT AT BIRTH	ELEMENT IN 2012	LUCK RATING
LIFE FORCE	EARTH	EARTH	O
HEALTH LUCK	EARTH	WATER	OO
FINANCE LUCK	METAL	WATER	OX
SUCCESS LUCK	FIRE	WOOD	OOO
SPIRIT ESSENCE	FIRE	FIRE	X

WATER SHEEP
9 YEARS OLD

TYPE OF LUCK	ELEMENT AT BIRTH	ELEMENT IN 2012	LUCK RATING
LIFE FORCE	EARTH	EARTH	O
HEALTH LUCK	WOOD	WATER	OOO
FINANCE LUCK	WATER	WATER	O
SUCCESS LUCK	FIRE	WOOD	OOO
SPIRIT ESSENCE	FIRE	FIRE	X

Chapter Three

PERSONALIZING YOUR FENG SHUI LUCK IN 2012

Individualized Directions to Protect Your Good Feng Shui

In 2012 the Sheep's fortune benefits from its much improved Life Force and Inner Chi Essence and for many of you born in the Sheep year, 2012 also bring improved Success and Financial luck. This means that the year will see you moving ahead professionally or in your business with less hindrances and difficulties, and also leading to you achieving all you set out to achieve. There are however some powerful conflict bringing energies which you really must subdue, both with feng shui and with more patience on your part.

For the Sheep, the Dragon Year brings a sense of being pulled in different directions; you get stressed out a lot this year and will find it a challenge balancing the different hats you wear.

For many Sheep, the year poses several dilemma issues and you will be forced to choose between alternative courses of action. And your choices may not all be as good as you might wish. The tradeoffs you face be quite tough, so success comes, but it is not straightforward; and neither will the decisions you have to make be easy.

Then there is the matter of stress-related anger and impatience. Unless you make a big effort to keep your angry reactions to a minimum, the "killing" stars near you might cause you to do, or say things you might well regret.

Indeed, this year, even the smallest of things can cause you to lose your cool and flare up. Others working with you could find it hard to work with you. This can lead to repercussions that could be unpleasant. That is when it might be helpful to remember that your intolerant mood is due the discordant energies of the year afflicting you; feng shui winds cause you to be quite quarrelsome and definitely very hostile.

It is likely that those near and dear to you suffer the most. If this leads to separation or unhappiness, it really would be a shame, because usually, the Sheep person is controlled and very loving and patient.

Feng shui this year thus has to focus on keeping discordant vibes from spoiling things for you. Taken to their extreme conflict energy can also lead to litigation, violence or worse, can also be tragic. So 2012 is a year to think of consequences; never forget that your actions and your words have consequences which may not always be pleasant or easy to deal with.

The key to a harmonious and successful year lies in keeping conflicts and hostile energies firmly under control and, not allowing anger to degenerate into violence and tragedy.

The Sheep's main problem comes from the number 3 star occupying its home location. At its worst, the number 3 star can cause a total reversal of your fortunes. The 3 star also makes you argumentative, and makes others treat you with impatience. This is sure to rile you, so the number 3 star MUST be subdued.

The feng shui to keeping conflict influences under control is to bring fresh new Fire element energy into the place of the Sheep i.e. to the SW1 location. Keep this part of your home and this corner of all the rooms you frequently occupy brightly lit. Never let the light get dim in these corners.

In terms of feng shui luck, what the Sheep should do immediately is to give the home a thorough spring cleaning, making sure the energies in all your living and work spaces are not left to stagnate. This is equivalent of the five minutes of body shaking each morning, something which experts on energy highly recommend to ensure the chi within our bodies are kept moving each day when we wake up.

Shift your furniture to move your space chi. This allows air to flow through the hidden spaces of nooks and corners, and when you are done, move your furniture back. Use this exercise to clean hard to reach spaces. This is a powerful re energising ritual which encourages energy to move, thus creating yang chi and bringing vibrant new energy into your home. This should get you ready for the new year; this shaking and moving ritual also makes sure your life does not stagnate and that you will continue to grow steadily and with vigor. It may sound simple, but this simple is effective and powerful.

Next, you can customize the feng shui of your space, by activating the astrological location of your animal sign and by using compass directions feng shui to maximise your luck for the year.

MAKING SHEEP'S SOUTHWEST 1 LOCATION AUSPICIOUS

The location of the Sheep is Southwest 1. You must know exactly where this part of your home is; this is your Sheep location which you must pay special attention to. You must never for whatever reason at all leave this corner dirty, cluttered or worse filled with rotting materials.

This part of the home must reflect your care and attention and it should definitely not be your store room, nor your toilet and also try not to do any cooking in this part of the house or room. It is vital to bring correct feng shui inputs to this part of the home, as well as to this Southwest 1 corner of all the rooms frequently used by you. The element of this space is Earth while the incoming feng shui wind here in 2012 is Wood and because this is an afflicted element bringing quarrelsome vibes this year, it is necessary to keep Wood subdued. Unfortunately, Wood overcomes Earth, and this does not benefit the Sheep. So what is needed here is Fire energy. The element of Fire will exhaust the Wood and thus subdue the conflict energies brought by the number 3, and Fire also enhances the home location element of Earth.

> The key to increasing the Sheep's good fortunes in 2012 is to increase the supply of **Fire element** in the Southwest 1 sector of the home.

The Earth element energy here in the Southwest 1 sector benefits the Sheep whose own element is also Earth, so this sector's energy helps to bring harmony luck to the Sheep. Strengthening Earth here is therefore also beneficial for Sheep. Significantly also, Fire is the element that is missing from the chart, so any enhancement of Fire here will also be very beneficial.

ENHANCER FOR THE SOUTHWEST: One thing we really want to recommend is to place a really meaningful lampshade here - with either white or yellow light and with the powerful *Hum* seed syllable on the shade. This will soothe the Sheep's state of mind and bring in the feel-good factor. Doing so not only reinforces the Sheep's inner essence and good fortune, but Fire energy also subdues the conflict star afflicting the Sheep.

ENHANCING YOUR PERSONAL LO SHU NUMBER

The Lo Shu numbers of Sheep for both Men and Women are either 3, 6 or 9. Each of these three numbers signify each of the three 20 year periods in the feng shui cycle of 180 years. Which number you have as your Lo Shu depends on your year of birth. And these are summarised in the charts in this part of the book.

Your personalised Lo Shu number interacts with the Lo Shu number of the year, and your good luck during the year is either enhanced or afflicted by the way the numbers interact. The Lo Shu number

BIRTH YEAR	ELEMENT SHEEP	AGE	LO SHU NUMBER AT BIRTH
1943	WATER SHEEP	69	3
1955	WOOD SHEEP	57	9
1967	FIRE SHEEP	46	6
1979	EARTH SHEEP	33	3
1991	METAL SHEEP	21	9

of 2012 is the white number 6, while the Lo Shu numbers of those born in Sheep years are shown in the table above. Note that this order of the numbers 3, 9 or 6 refer to both men and women...

Sheep with Birth Lo Shu of 3 (affecting the 69 and 33 year old Sheep)

The number 3 is softened by the number 6 which is the Lo Shu number of the year. This combination brings better diplomatic skills to the 69 and 33 year old Sheep, who can be intolerant and quite unyielding this year. This helps them avoid troubles erupting into volcanoes! The Lo Shu of 3 makes these Sheep arrogant and rather quarrelsome. They tend to be edgy and unbending, and also quite authoritative, and in 2012, these tendencies get pronounced because they are also afflicted by the negative side of the number 3 star. Fortunately, their Lo Shu number syncs well with the Lo Shu of the year, so wise counsel is available to them and perhaps even an influential mentor to bring them good advice. A special word of advice to the **33 year old Sheep** is to take things easy and not work as though as you are so driven. Take time to breathe and to smell the flowers.

Sheep with Birth Lo Shu of 9 (affecting the 57 and 21 year old Sheep)

The Lo Shu number of this Sheep is 9 and its relationship with the number 6 is neutral but both are lucky numbers that bring different aspects of good fortune luck so this is a good and lucky year for these Sheep born people.

The 9 with 6 is an excellent indication in terms of increasing your wealth luck. There will be unexpected developments that lead to some exciting possibilities as the 6 brings luck from the heavens – this is a year when many opportunities can manifest, but do be discerning when trying to take advantage of these opportunities.

Curb your enthusiasm and always use your head over your emotional reactions. In the euphoria of new pathways, you can succumb to carelessness and impulsiveness.

But make no bones about it. The combination of 9 with 6 is very promising; just be careful and not take action without careful thought first. **Protect the Southeast** of your home with a water feature and also place a bright light here. This will do wonders for your recognition luck.

Sheep with Birth Lo Shu of 6 (affecting the 8 and 46 year old Sheep)

The number 6 gets auspiciously doubled by the number 6 of the year and this emphasizes all the characteristics attached to this Lo Shu number affecting the **46 year old Fire Sheep** and the **8 year old Water Sheep** who both have this as their birth Lo Shu number. So in 2012, their attributes of high intelligence, as well as help from unexpected sources and great networking luck bring them some truly big opportunities.

For the 46 year olds, business luck gets enhanced as they start to catch the eye of important people. It also indicates that they might move into a new house this year, although it would have been better done before the year changed i.e. in the Year of the Rabbit.

This is not a great year to uproot yourself by moving location or country. It is also not a good year to change jobs. If you have plans to make big changes better to wait till the following year. Protect the Southeast of your home with remedies to dissolve the influence of the 5 yellow and also place water in this corner.

FINETUNING SHEEP'S DIRECTION IN 2012

The Eight Mansions formula divides people into East and West groups, with each group having their own lucky and unlucky directions. To use Eight Mansions, you first need to determine your auspicious directions and then make it a point to always face at least one of your good directions while working, negotiating, sleeping, eating or dating.

There are different lucky directions for men and women, and these are calculated using their lunar year of birth. Just doing this faithfully, using a good compass to determine the directions, will bring you instant good feng shui. This is also one of the easiest formulas of feng shui to use and the one in which you are least likely to make a mistake. Study your good and bad luck directions from the charts here. Note that the directions are different for each of the Kua numbers, and also note that the order of the Kua numbers are different for the different Male and female Sheep.

AUSPICIOUS DIRECTIONS FOR SHEEP FEMALES

Sheep women with Kua numbers 3 or 9 belong to the East group of lucky directions and they benefit from facing East or South in 2012 as these are directions that benefit them and are not afflicted in 2012.

The best direction for East group people this year for romance and good relationship luck is East, which has the auspicious peach blossom star of 4. This star also brings excellent scholastic luck.

BIRTH YEAR	AGE	ELEMENT/ KUA	HEALTH DIRECTION	SUCCESS DIRECTION	LOVE & FAMILY DIRECTION	PERSONAL GROWTH DIRECTION
1943	69	WATER/3	N	S	SE	E
1955	57	WOOD/6	NE	W	SW	NW
1967	46	FIRE/9	SE	E	N	S
1979	33	EARTH/3	N	S	SE	E
1991	21	METAL/6	NE	W	SW	NW

Those of you whose Success direction is South also benefit this year because the South is blessed with strong victory luck this year. This facing direction is especially suitable for the **33 year old Sheep lady** who is just embarking on a career or in a serious relationship. For her, facing South will bring excellent relationship and success luck.

East group women Sheep should not face North, as this is an afflicted direction that brings illness and general feelings of apathy and lethargy. You should also avoid facing the Southeast which is very badly afflicted in 2012.

The **57 year old Wood Lady Sheep** and **21 year old Sheep girl** belong to the West group. These ladies should definitely tap the very lucky West direction this year as it is from the West that powerful good fortune comes in 2012.

But you must both avoid your other lucky directions of Southwest and Northwest because these two directions are seriously afflicted with the conflict and the cheating stars respectively. Instead, it is better for you to face the other good luck direction i.e. the Northeast which benefits from the luck of future prosperity.

AUSPICIOUS DIRECTIONS FOR SHEEP MEN

BIRTH YEAR	AGE	ELEMENT/ KUA	HEALTH DIRECTION	SUCCESS DIRECTION	LOVE & FAMILY DIRECTION	PERSONAL GROWTH DIRECTION
1943	69	WATER/3	N	S	SE	E
1955	57	WOOD/9	SE	E	N	S
1967	46	FIRE/6	NE	W	SW	NW
1979	33	EARTH/3	N	S	SE	E
1991	21	METAL/9	SE	E	N	S

Advice for Sheep men is similar as that offered to the Lady Sheep. Once you know if you are East or West group, you will know which directions to tap into and which to avoid in 2012. East Group Sheep men have Kua numbers 3 and 9, while the West group gentlemen Sheep have Kua number 6. Note that those of you whose Success direction is East can face East this year and doing so brings also good health and good relationship luck. It is the Southeast direction that you need to avoid facing! The other good direction for East group guys is South which is also the Success direction of the **69 year old Water Sheep gentleman** and the **33 year old Sheep young**

man. This indicates that these two Sheep enjoy better luck than the others as South is a winning direction in 2012. The young man especially will benefit from facing South if he is looking to find a meaningful job to get him started onto a fine career.

The West group Sheep gentlemen (**36 year old Fire Sheep**) are advised to tap strongly into the West direction and to give the Southwest and Northwest a miss this year. But facing Northeast brings the luck of longer-term wealth-building luck.

IMPROVING SHEEP'S FENG SHUI LUCK IN 2012

Note that the quickest way to attract good fortune is to tap your personalized lucky directions, as long as you make certain your lucky directions are not afflicted in 2012.

Facing a direction that brings you good fortune and which is also in sync with the year is the easiest way to ensure good feng shui for the year. Note that even if you cannot tap your best direction you must at least avoid facing directions that are unlucky for you or that are afflicted in 2012.

Attracting Success

Sheep with Kua number 6 should position their sitting direction at work to face West or Northeast as discussed earlier. Those with Kua 3 or 9 should face South this year or East for improved relationship luck. Taking note of the directions that are best for you, try to arrange your desk to face the appropriate lucky direction; but also take note of the taboo desk alignments to avoid; to start, always look at what is behind you.

Do not get hurt by something behind you while focusing on facing a lucky direction. Watch your back! So…

- ► Avoid a window behind you especially if your office or home work area is located several levels up a multi-level building.
- ► Avoid having the door into your room being placed behind you.
- ► Avoid being directly in the line of fire of sharp edges or tables, corners and protruding corners. And definitely DO NOT place your desk at funny angles just to tap into your lucky direction. This can backfire, bringing misfortune luck instead.

Ensuring Good Health

An excellent way to ensure good health in 2012 is to capture your individual good health direction. The secret of good health luck is to sleep with your head pointed to your Health direction or at least one of the four auspicious directions. You should ensure that your Health direction does not suffer from any affliction in 2012.

Sheep should note that the two West group directions that are hurt by the feng shui winds of 2012 are Southwest and Northwest. These two powerful directions are afflicted by hostile energies so even if they are listed as your Health direction, do not face these directions or sleep with your head pointing to either of these directions.

As for the Sheep men and women who belong to the East group, note that the North is seriously afflicted by the illness star, so on no accounts should you face North.

Likewise, the Southeast is seriously hurt by the five yellow, which also manifests illness of the most severe kind. This too is a direction to be avoided. Remember that sleeping right is one of the easiest of feng shui ways to ensure good health. This, plus making certain you are not afflicted by the annual and monthly illness star numbers, is what will help ensure you do not succumb to sickness.

For all Sheep, please note that the months of **February**, **August** and **November** are when you must take extra good care of your health as these are the months when you are the most vulnerable.

In these months do wear the **gold wu lou** as this is an excellent amulet against getting sick. You can also wear the **Medicine Buddha bracelet** or **moving mantra watch** which was made precisely to guard against falling ill to epidemics or viruses.

The Medicine Buddha moving mantra watch is an excellent antidote to health woes when the illness star makes an appearance in your chart.

In the Bedroom

To enjoy good feng shui always be sensitive to the way your bed is oriented and positioned in the bedroom.

A golden rule is that beds should always be positioned against a solid wall, and should not share a wall with a toilet or bathroom on the other side. This gives you the solid support you need and the headboard forms a symbolic protective aura that guards you while you sleep. So it is always preferable to have a headboard.

You should make sure never to have toilets on the other side of the wall where your bed is placed. The toilet symbolically flushes away all bad luck but to have it directly behind you while you sleep suggests that all your good luck gets flushed away as well.

Beds that are placed against a wall with space around it are always more auspicious than beds that are wedged tight into corners.

Do make sure there are no heavy beams above you as you sleep and no sharp columns hitting at you from protruding corners and cupboards. These cause illness. And do take note of window views. If you can see blue skies at nights and there is a clear view it is both healthy and auspicious - so also are views of vibrantly growing trees although these should never be too near to your window. But do make sure not to be looking at a dead tree stump or a hostile looking tree outside as these can bring illness into the bedroom.

Becoming a Star at School or College

To bring good feng shui luck to the **21 year old Sheep** who is probably still at College, note first that the man has Kua 9 and is East group while the girl has Kua 6 and is West group.

> In 2012 the young Sheep girl can benefit hugely from sitting facing South which is your personal growth direction. But you can also face East, because the literary and scholastic star has flown here this year. So for the Sheep girl, facing South or East are beneficial.

The young Sheep man belonging to West group should face West or Northeast and although this may not be the best direction to benefit from your own personal growth luck, these two directions are excellent for bringing present and future success.

Attracting Romance into your Life

If you are looking for love, romance or marriage, there can be good news for Sheep belonging to the East group because the *Peach Blossom Star* lands in the East in 2012. This is makes it a powerful love direction for activating marriage luck this year. So no matter your age, irrespective of whether you have been married before, this year you can set the energy moving to bring you good marriage luck simply by placing a **bejeweled Rabbit** in the East!

For West group Sheep, we advise tapping the West sector by placing a **bejeweled Rooster** in here because the luck of the Rooster is very strong this year, so even though the Rooster is not your peach blossom animal, this can be a good way to bring you romance luck. Likewise wearing the **Phoenix scarf** also brings romance and love your way!

Wearing the phoenix scarf activates love and romance luck for the Sheep person.

Chapter Four

RELATIONSHIP LUCK FOR 2012

The Sheep should focus on work to dispel & dissolve afflicted relationship luck

Each year, we all react to the people around us differently, and depending on what our sign is, we can be more accommodating in one year and less so in another. How you treat and respond to those you love - your family, lovers, spouse or children - and to those you work with - colleagues, employees, bosses and business associates - depend very much on your relationship energies during the year. This will influence your tolerance levels and your patience. Some years you can be very loving and forgiving, feeling at ease with yourself and with the world, and other years you can be intolerant and impatient and not easy to relate to.

COMPATIBILITY
WITH EACH ANIMAL SIGN

COMPATIBILITY	LUCK OUTLOOK IN 2012
SHEEP with RAT	Potentially a prickly relationship
SHEEP with OX	Strongly quarrelsome with conflict energy
SHEEP with TIGER	Tendency to fight and quarrel a great deal
SHEEP with RABBIT	Keeping your latent jealousy under control
SHEEP with DRAGON	Misunderstandings cause tensions
SHEEP with SNAKE	Both sides stay wary of one another
SHEEP with HORSE	Strong ties marred by intermittent hostility
SHEEP with SHEEP	A noisy relationship that cannot satisfy
SHEEP with MONKEY	Misunderstandings hurt each other
SHEEP with ROOSTER	A soul mate who has time for you
SHEEP with DOG	A good and loyal friend who brings solace
SHEEP with BOAR	This pair of allies try to find common ground

The Sheep usually tends to be soft spoken and rarely loses its cool. The Sheep is also excellent at hiding whatever negative feelings it may be feeling. But in 2012, it is quite the opposite, and not just because of the hostile star - also because of the yearly killing energies brought by the 24 Mountains Compass Wheel.

The energies of the year cause aggravations and obstacles and this hits even the Sheep's relationships with its special astrological allies and friends. As a result, Sheep will be difficult with friends and family, and socializing brings out latent mental baggage. The Sheep is not feeling at all friendly this year.

The Sheep lacks patience in 2012 and there could even be direct confrontations with others that will cause your mind to get disturbed. It is a good idea to work at suppressing the urge to flare up and avoid succumbing to anger and impatience.

The Sheep personality is usually alien to moodswings, so if you let yourself get angry too often, it is sure to affect your equilibrium. This will take its toll on those near and dear to you. The year's energies are still discordant and it is better not to roll into the energy of the year, so do make a strong effort to stay cool. Even if you do not feel like going out much, with whoever you do socialize with, try to be happy and jovial. Do not give in to dark moods and depression.

The Sheep is in its element when it is deep into a special project, as being focused and single-minded comes easily to you. In 2012, the Year of the Dragon, there are good opportunities that come your way, and those who direct their energies inward, zeroing in on matters which engage you totally, will find this turning out to be a good year.

In 2012, things work out more beneficial for you if you work alone, and at your own pace. You will get much more achieved this way than in too many "group situations" and it is also better for your peace of mind.

Do not berate yourself if you seem lethargic at the thought of socializing and networking. It is just as beneficial to stay home, mind the kids, mind the store and allow your own creative juices to flow. This is a great year to be something of a loner. Do note however that animal signs generally interact in a positive way with their Zodiac allies, their secret friend and astrological soulmates. But the extent of affinity does magnify or get reduced according to the feng shui energy of each sign in different years. So while it is absolutely important to know about these groupings, it is equally important to finetune the level of affinity enjoyed each year.

For the Sheep, this is not a year that particularly favors relationships, even with very compatible people. You are not in the mood to socialize.

Each sign has another sign with whom it may be difficult to feel much warmth towards - we call the energy that flow between them arrows of antagonism. It can be troublesome when someone you care for or have just met and feel attracted to belongs to an animal sign that is supposedly your astrological "enemy" - these are signs placed directly opposite you in the Astrology Wheel.

But like it or not, these "arrows" indicate longterm incompatibility, and for the Sheep, these feelings of antagonism to its astrological enemy the Ox could well get magnified this year.

Auspicious Crosses

It is always preferred for siblings to be astrological
allies, rather than astrological enemies. So planning
your family according to astrological guidelines has
its benefits. There is however an astrological secret
associated with "enemy signs" and this gives families
the key to unlocking strong lucky vibes for the entire
family. This requires the presence of what is generally
referred to as the *Auspicious Crosses* formed by four
members within a family unit.

**These Crosses exist in a family
when there are two specific pairs
of antagonistic siblings e.g. if
you, the Sheep also has an Ox,
your astrological enemy in your
family then you have one pair of
antagonistic arrow in the family.**

But with this pair you can create the highly auspicious
Earth Cross simply by having a **Dragon** and a
Dog also in the family. This Cross brings excellent
grounding energy to any family which ahs it and in
2012 the Earth element brings **wealth and prosperity
luck**. Note however that for the Cross to work, all four
of you should be living in the same house and under
the same roof.

THE EARTH CROSS

The Earth Cross activates wealth and prosperity luck for the grouping and reduces the effect of the arrows of antagonism between opposite animal signs. The Earth Cross is made up of the four animals of the Earth element - the Ox, Dragon, Sheep and Dog.

So for instance, if you are the father or the mother in the family, as the Sheep, your family unit can create the auspicious Earth Cross which comprises an Ox, a Dog, and a Dragon with the Sheep. This requires that you are married to one of these signs and if you have two children belonging to the other two signs, you would have created within your family a very powerful Earth Cross.

So if in your family you already have the first three signs between you, and there is no end of squabbling between your opposing astrological signs, you can keep this option in mind.

The Sheep's Astrological Allies

Your allies are the Rabbit and the Boar. In 2012 you are aided by the powerful energy of your ally the Rabbit with whose association you get to enhance your charisma and aura. This adds to your popularity and makes others attracted to you. It is the Rabbit who is the shining star in your trinity of allies, so it is beneficial for you to stick close to this ally. The danger for 2012 is that jealousy vibes could arise, causing you to have real differences with your strong and powerful ally. So the Sheep needs to work at subduing them. Your secret friend is the Horse and with the Horse you have better compatibility in 2012.

PAIRINGS OF
SECRET FRIENDS

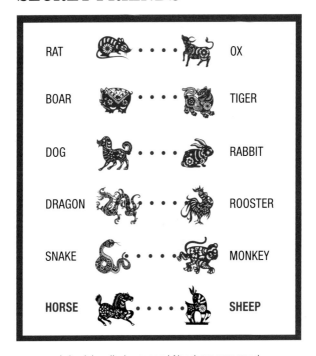

RAT	OX
BOAR	TIGER
DOG	RABBIT
DRAGON	ROOSTER
SNAKE	MONKEY
HORSE	**SHEEP**

Animal signs that are secret friends are very good
for each other and you can help each other even without knowing.
The Sheep's secret friend is the Ox.

This is a year when your ally the Rabbit's strength is very obvious and your hostile energy is very strong, so Rabbit's success may not sit well on you. The Sheep is influenced by the hostile winds of the number 3 star, so feng shui winds tend to foster a certain coolness even to your own allies. This is neither beneficial nor wise. **Wear red** to keep hostile tendencies under control.

Sheep

Rabbit

AFFINITY TRIANGLE OF DIPLOMATS

Boar

The Rabbit is the luckiest of the trinity of Sheep, Rabbit and Boar this year. So it benefits Sheep to stick close to your ally the Rabbit.

Other than that, the Sheep's luck is forward looking this year, so it is really a matter of keeping impatience under check and of consciously welcoming every new friendship with confidence. Keep feelings of envy and jealousy under wraps and look within yourself to bring out the lighter, brighter side to make the most of all the relationships in your life.

Your luck, and that of the Boar, your other ally are very mixed in 2012 so there will be months of unstable luck that get you down. Your serious affliction is of course the quarrelsome number 3 star.

This will explain your mood swings and hostile nature and you should try to bear with it. Unfortunately your other ally the Boar is also afflicted by the violent robbery star number 7 which can bring severe and traumatic loss in 2012.

So really, both you and your other ally the Boar need to turn to the Rabbit, who is the hero of the trinity this year.

In terms of compatibility, you should make an effort to try and get along well with each of your astrological allies as this lends the three of you good synergistic strength resulting in better trust and greater friendship with one another. To harness maximum benefit from your affinity allies, it is beneficial to carry the symbolic image of your allies.

In 2012 the best for the Sheep is to carry the image of the **Rabbit** and also the **Horse** your secret friend!

Carry your Crest of Allies

What will be great is for you to wear or display your allies/secret friend Crest which we have specially designed to place close to you to remind you of their significance in strengthening your energies during the year. The great significance of activating your astrological grouping is often overlooked by many people so do use the **Crest wallet** or **brooch** not just to remind you but also to activate the essence of the trinity. For the Sheep, what would benefit you is the Crest of the Rabbit/Boar/Sheep.

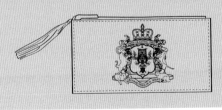

The Sheep and both its allies are usually known for their gentle diplomatic approach to getting along with people as well as their stoic handling of life's issues. You are the **Diplomats of the Zodiac** and are usually able to absorb whatever difficulties come your way with a philosophical mindset. Your trinity of allies make good homemakers, so managing the family comes easily to you.

In 2012, try and access these inbuilt attributes. You possess great determination and moral courage, so it should not be too difficult to rise above petty anger and aggravations and let your better self emerge. Together, the three of you can achieve much.

Although you each have your own outer and inner strengths, it is the Sheep who has the most staying power. The Boar has an admirable store of joy de vivre and this can be infectious. The Rabbit is more ambitious, especially in 2012, so you could be at cross purposes trying to bond with this particular ally.

The Sheep, Rabbit and Boar are silently confident and calm personalities. They usually come across soft and yielding, but have an inner core of steel. Once they make up their minds, it is almost impossible to hope to change them.

This is a group of people who look out for each other. They may not appear as loyal as the other grouping led by Tiger, but they are effective and selective in the way they extend out a helping hand to one another. They are not as competitive as some of the other signs and they are also quite easy going, being nowhere near as difficult to handle as others. As a result, many people like having this trinity of signs working in committees or within specific teams in a work environment.

Sheep, Rabbit and Boar allies and always look out for one another.

SHEEP WITH SHEEP
In 2012 a noisy relationship that cannot satisfy

When two people of the Sheep sign get together, their similar natures instantly make for a restful and cordial relationship, except that in 2012, with both of you falling under the influence of the number 3 star of arguments and misunderstandings, you might not see quite as much goodwill as you would expect to see.

Usually, however competitive, pressures rarely come into the picture for a pair of two Sheep, and there is little to cause tension or lead to prickly friction between these two. It is just that the year's energies affecting them are discordant and not conducive to a happy domestic situation.

Nevertheless, if already a couple, their common interests and similar long term goals make it easy for them to build a meaningful life together. They also work well together, and in a good year can actually achieve quite a great deal. There is genuine support of each other in this relationship. However, when things between them get too noisy and there are too many

133

arguments driving them apart - as could happen this year - then satisfaction and happiness flies out the window.

> What could work against this pair are their "light ears". They are easily in influenced by others and in a year when the possibility of misunderstandings arising is quite high, this could lead to problems coming between this pair.

Sheep signs can often lack the strength or shrewdness to see through hidden agendas, and from this perspective, others could very well come between them. As a result, their union with their spouse or partnership with their business associate might suffer a breakdown in communications.

When they have second thoughts on important matters, Sheep people tend to prevaricate. This tendency towards indecision can and will lead to some quite negative consequences this year.

Do be alert to this happening to your relationship. You may be good together, but you need to be more steadfast in your commitment. You also need to be less fickle and less changeable, especially when it comes to committing to another person. This year 2012, the

Sheep person has the tendency to chop and change as their inner spiritual essence is not at a good level. This makes them waver and hesitate when they should be firm and decisive.

Besides, apart from being hit by the hostile star in the feng shui chart, the Sheep also has to deal with a conflict star brought by the 24 Mountains Compass, so in a sense there is a double whammy affecting the Sheep's relationships luck. Knowing this should really make you more determined than ever to stay strong. When things go wrong, it is better to look for solutions than to look for someone close to hang your frustration on.

Note that the Sheep in 2012 can succumb to sudden bouts of jealousy and envy. If this happens, it is sure to rock the boat for you. An unreasonable kind of possessiveness can very easily get out of hand. So do be alert to anything like this getting the better of you this year.

SHEEP WITH RABBIT
In 2012 keeping your latent jealousy under control

There is no doubt that these two are allies who easily see each other as kindred spirits.

But in 2012, there is a big difference in the attitude of these two signs. Rabbit is relaxed and confident, while Sheep tends to be stressed out and hostile. It is not surprising that resentment of some kind and at some will creep in to mess up this fine relationship.

You need to hang in there with each other! This is a pairing where ordinarily you would be waxing lyrical about each other and also enthusiastically digging in to all the fine things that life brings your way.

Ordinarily also you would be enjoying the good things of life together, finding beauty and value in the skies and the mountains. You both like exactly the same things. You enjoy going to museums, attending auctions, going shopping, finding gems in flea markets - i.e. simple outings which allow two people to enjoy each other.

(*Jealousy Could Creep In* ★★★)

You are two people who can get your highs discovering restaurants and fun places thereby creating your own world where love flows freely between them. You also get bored by the same kinds of things and are stimulated by similar experiences. So here we see an emotional and artistic affinity flowering into deep and abiding love.

But in this Year of the Dragon, things do not appear so hunky dory at all. There will develop a hidden resentment and even touches of envy and jealousy - which can cause both parties to get tired and exhausted of one another. Eventually, however, if they can survive a year of quarrels and misunderstandings, this couple are certain to become soul mates again, capable of bringing great happiness to each other.

To them, the environment is secondary and work can never take precedence over their concern for each other's happiness. They are genuine allies, looking out for each other and easily creating rapport and comradeship.

But tempers flare easily and anger simmers beneath the surface over seemingly unimportant things, as hostile energies of the year take their toll on you both.

It is advisable to each do your own thing this year, and the less said between each other the better. The Sheep's life is made difficult by the hostile star 3. There is also the yearly killing & yearly conflict stars brought by the 24 Mountains Compass, so this is not an easy year for Sheep.

The good thing is that the Rabbit is meanwhile riding along with none of the stresses afflicting its ally, hence better for this pair to take things easy and let the relationship survive through the year.

 FENG SHUI ADVICE: The Sheep might want to consider **wearing red** and carrying the **Magic Diagram Red Sword Mirror** to subdue the hostility star. This will smooth your relations during the year and reduce misunderstandings with others.

Usually a good match, but this year things could get a little difficult for this pair.

SHEEP WITH BOAR
In 2012 this pair of allies try to find common ground

The Boar is the other ally of the Sheep, so there is good affinity between them. This is a sign with whom the Sheep has no trouble bonding with. Except that in 2012, the Sheep is not exactly the easiest person to get along with and hence could prove to be something of an aggravation to the mild-mannered Boar. Both will try to overlook their differences even when these arise too frequently to overlook.

There will thus be misunderstandings through the year but there is no denying that here is a well suited and happy couple whose eager approach to life finds good chemistry developing between each other.

Happily, their natural affinity is infectious and this innate goodwill is sure to help them successfully overcome obstacles arising through the year. They do have great and obvious love for each other, and their inborn niceness to each other makes them restful and comfortable in one another's presence. Theirs is thus an easy relationship and it would be true to say they are so good for one another that even with problems coming between them, their long-term commitment will not be affected.

They will find joy in 2012 pursuing the same things and providing companionship to each other; this is not difficult for them as they will be drawn to the same things and motivated by the same causes.

As a couple or family, they find it easy to plan outings and holidays. If they get into a work relationship with each other, they will be supportive and helpful, easily forging a partnership and working in tandem without too much effort at all. If they are married, it should be a happy union.

The Sheep and the Boar make up two thirds of the group of allies described as the **Diplomats of the Zodiac**. They share many similar attributes and their lifestyle mirrors a desire for a life of quiet elegance. They communicate easily, speak and think on the same wavelength and are sensitive of each other's needs. This is a couple who are "touchy"'and "feely". They love to hug and they are also easily demonstrative. Should they be courting, they are likely to wear their hearts on their sleeves.

So despite the year putting strains on the Sheep causing it to get in to mood swings and occasionally succumbing to anger moments, the year should prove to be quite good to this pair. There will be much happiness flowing between them, especially if they pursue paths of spirituality that enable them to access the heaven luck that pervades the year.

In this, the Boar's energy is helped by the **Star of Heavenly Seal** brought to it by the 24 mountains Compass. This pair can also carry the **Heaven Seal** to invoke the help of heaven energy on their relationship with each other.

The Boar and Sheep are astrological allies and make a great long-term couple. There coukld be misunderstandings this year, but nothing that cannot get resolved.

The Sheep's Secret Friend & Zodiac Housemate

In addition to astrological allies, the Sheep also has a *Secret Friend* and *Zodiac Housemate* with whom it creates an incredibly special relationship; one that is even more influential than what it can have with either of its astrological allies.

Sometimes one's secret friend and Zodiac housemate are different signs but in the case of the Sheep sign, your secret friend is also your Zodiac Housemate. This is the sign of the Horse and so you will find that the Horse will bring up incredibly tender feelings within you.

You will most likely feel exceptionally close to the Horse sign who can easily eventually become your soul mate and probably your best friend as well.

The Sheep and Horse have the potential to forge an extremely close and very compatible relationship with each other.

They have a lot of time for one another and there will flow between them a very sweet sense of comradeship that generates precious moments and happiness vibes.

Even when they disagree, they are still able to stay close. For them there will rarely be shouting matches. This pair fights silently! Secret friends nurture one another, bringing out each other's strengths and strong points. It is always beneficial to enter in any kind of relationship with one's secret friend.

As for the Zodiac's Housemate connection, this likewise generates a **flow of hidden strengths** and skills between Sheep and Horse. As partners in love, or in business, or as team mates, they create a powerful alliance which can be very successful commercially.

THE 6 DIFFERENT ZODIAC HOUSE PAIRINGS

ANIMALS	YIN/YANG	ZODIAC HOUSE	SKILLS UNLEASHED
RAT	YANG	HOUSE OF CREATIVITY & CLEVERNESS	The Rat initiates
OX	YIN		The Ox completes
TIGER	YANG	HOUSE OF GROWTH & DEVELOPMENT	The Tiger employs force
RABBIT	YIN		The Rabbit uses diplomacy
DRAGON	YANG	HOUSE OF MAGIC & SPIRITUALITY	The Dragon creates magic
SNAKE	YIN		The Snake creates mystery
HORSE	YANG	HOUSE OF PASSION & SEXUALITY	The Horse embodies male energy
SHEEP	YIN		The Sheep is the female energy
MONKEY	YANG	HOUSE OF CAREER & COMMERCE	The Monkey creates strategy
ROOSTER	YIN		The Rooster gets things moving
DOG	YANG	HOUSE OF DOMESTICITY	The Dog works to provide
BOAR	YIN		The Boar enjoys what is created

SHEEP WITH HORSE
In 2012, strong ties marred by intermittent hostility

In 2012 the two signs of Sheep and Horse, although astrologically closely linked, could clash with one another. Despite their strong ties, both signs get hit by strongly negative stars brought by the 24 Mountains Compass. The Sheep is sitting on yearly killing stars while Horse is sitting and flanked by Three Killings stars.

It would appear that together or individually they have a lot of their hands. They will need an extraordinary store of patience and goodwill to ride through a stormy 2012. And even with strong feng shui cures in place, it is likely the there will be intermittent hostility causing unhappiness and a great deal of aggravation.

The Zodiac is bullish about a Sheep and Horse pairing as this couple are not just "secret friends" but are also great soulmates as they share the same Zodiac house, that of *Sexuality and Passion*, with the Horse exuding the male yang energy and the Sheep creating the

145

female yin energy. In Zodiac terms, this translates to suggest complete compatibility. They have a special relationship that is strong and enduring and also they can last the long haul.

The Horse and Sheep have the ability to make each other extremely happy. They think in the same way and physically they are also very compatible. They are able to please each other and to establish good foundations for long term happiness. Their attraction is rooted in their attitudes which complement each other.

The Sheep and Horse are extremely good together.
They are both physically and mentally compatible.

The Horse is forthright and courageous and the Sheep is steady and stable. The Horse also likes to lead and take charge and this too is fine with the gentle and pliable Sheep, although here the Sheep is the more skilful of the two. Between them is a big store of goodwill and pleasant interchange. There is little cause for conflict and since neither side is of a quarrelsome nature, life in the Sheep/Horse household is peaceful and potentially enriching as well.

If there are any differences between them, these arise from their different attitudes towards child care and bringing up the upkeep of their children. In this, the Horse takes a free-spirited approach encouraging independence. The Sheep tends to be more conservative and also less courageous and will tend to stress safety over risk taking. But these differences are easily resolved... especially in 2012 when the Sheep is more likely to have its way.

 FENG SHUI ADVICE: It is a good idea to strengthen your Sheep's immunity to the *hostility star* by placing **bright lights** in the Southwest to subdue the quarrelsome energy that pervades the Sheep's home sector in 2012. This will ease whatever conflicts erupt between this pair.

147

The Sheep's Astrological Enemy

Astrological feng shui relating to relationships and compatibility between the twelve animal signs must take note of one's "astrological enemy". Basically this is represented by the animal sign that directly confronts you on the Compass wheel. In the case of the Sheep, your astrological enemy is the Ox, so there is usually cross purpose communication going on between people born of these two signs. Very likely there is also very little in common between these two. Between siblings, two generations and between relatives, this can be very trying and could even lead to strong quarrels.

Latent hostility and tensions rear their ugly heads... although this can be assuaged and transformed into a powerful group of four. Do this by adding a **Dragon** and a **Dog** to the equation in which case the family as a unit will then create the **Earth Cross** of animal signs placed in the four secondary Earth element directions.

With the presence of this cosmic Cross, whatever animosity there is will transform into a potent combination of auspiciousness. This is not an easy thing to accomplish... although in the old days, wealthy Chinese families sometimes adopt a relative's child into the family on the advice of the family astrologer or feng shui expert.

SHEEP WITH OX
In 2012, quarrelsome with too much conflict energy

Whenever two animal signs confront each other in the astrological compass, like in the case of the Sheep and the Ox, they will always suggest the presence of latent hostility. This may not manifest every year or all the time, but it will cause the two personalities to be abrupt and impatient with one another.

From young, the Ox is instinctively wary of the Sheep, and if you are in a sibling relationship with a Sheep, it is unlikely that you will be close. Even if you are, you will in all likelihood grow apart as you mature.

In 2012, a good amount of this instinctive animosity surfaces strongly, with the Ox and the Sheep directly confronting each other with yearly conflict stars.

Feelings of anger and conflicts surface all through the year and any relationship between the two of you is not only harmful and unlucky for both, it can also cause real loss to both. It is really more advisable to stay out of each other's way; this way mistrust and anger has less of a chance to arise.

It does not matter what the nature of your relationship with each other may be; it is a year when animosities can break out into some kind of confrontation.

The *Star of Yearly Conflict* is one of the "killing stars" of the 24 Mountains Zodiac. It is not a friendly star and when two such stars are in confrontation, it really is better not to let it burst forth into anger and violence.

Should Sheep be having difficulties with an Ox spouse, or with a colleague or associate, our advice is for you to understand the energies of the year and to curb any urge to react too excessively should simmering animosity explode. Just walk away and calm down.

Here the problem lies more with you the Sheep because you are sitting on the *Star of Yearly Killing*, and the *Star of Conflict* is on its left. This makes the hostile energy stronger.

The relationship between the two of you is thus very strained, and can lead to anger and loud voices; but once you understand that this is all part of the astrological roadmap of animal signs, any resentment which might otherwise well up inside you should subside, at least a little.

Note however that arrows of antagonism between zodiac enemies tend to flare up through the year, gaining special potency during certain months so do practice tolerance, especially if you are in a competitive situation with a Ox at the work place or for someone's affections. i.e. you are love rivals. As colleagues in a work environment, you might find you have to make extra effort to curb anger rising.

If you are married to an Ox, and you are feeling dissatisfied, you have to accept that it is not easy to be as close as you might wish to be; it is not easy to be understanding or tolerant. It is also hard to go deep with each other.

But the Sheep can and does put up with the Ox and vice versa if the relationship is a hierarchical one. These are two practical down-to-earth signs and if the balance of power in the relationship leans towards one or the other, the reality of situations will cause both to subdue latent hostility.

The Chinese believe that when the Sheep and the Ox marry and the marriage lasts, there is potential for great good fortune in the union. This happens if they produce children or add to the family equation a Dragon and a Dog. This creates what is known as the **Earth Cross**, which is auspicious for the family as a unit. If these four signs are in your paht chee chart, it also indicates good luck for the family especially good luck related to the earth element. This is something that is definitely worth considering if you are in this position.

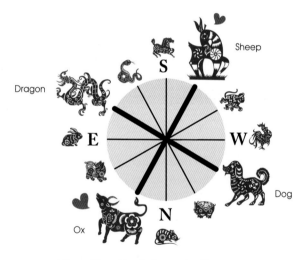

A Sheep/Ox pairing that are not getting along well can remedy this if a Dragon and Dog pair enter the equation. This can be the case for instance if Sheep/Ox parents have a Dragon child and a Dog child.

PAIRINGS OF
ASTROLOGICAL ENEMIES

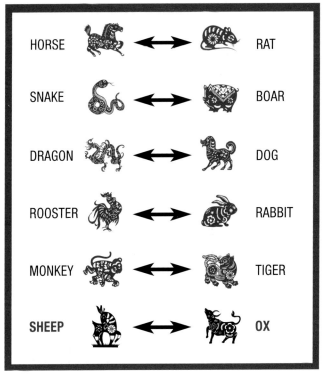

HORSE			RAT
SNAKE			BOAR
DRAGON			DOG
ROOSTER			RABBIT
MONKEY			TIGER
SHEEP			**OX**

Astrological "enemies" rarely make good long term partners whether in love or work relationships. The astrological enemy of the Sheep is the Ox.

SHEEP WITH RAT
In 2012, potentially a prickly relationship

Oh dear, the Rat will find the Sheep quite disagreeable this year! Already the differences between these two signs are big and wide ranging, but in 2012, the feng shui winds cause them to literally get sick with each other!

Sheep is extra quarrelsome this year and will be more short tempered than usual, while Rat is lethargic and easily bored. If they are a couple, married or living together, the year's energies really represent a recipe for disaster. If they have only just met, it is unlikely that either will want to take things too far.

The discomfort that Rat feels with this sign this year is easy to understand. The Sheep can be prickly and hostile, argumentative and unfriendly, influenced by the number 3 star. Conversation with each other leads nowhere and with Rat already feeling less than sprightly, it is unlikely it will make any kind of effort to meet Sheep halfway. So in terms of relationship luck, it would be safe to say that things will not work out well this year between this pair.

Should you the Sheep find yourself in a work or professional relationship with the Rat, the differences that surface between you both might just tip overboard and Rat will feel inclined to want out - either asking for a transfer or getting out of any project you may be working on together. It is not just boredom that sets in but during 2012, real differences crop up that lead to bad feeling, animosity and even hostility.

The Sheep is afflicted by the number 3 hostility star and this makes Sheep argumentative and uncompromising. In addition, Sheep is also afflicted by the *Yearly Killing Star* and remember, the year also has the *Star of Aggressive Sword*. So all in all, we are seeing the manifestation of some pretty violent and hostile energies converging around the aura of the Sheep.

It will take someone who is better disposed to Sheep to deal with its cocktail of hostile vibes. Certainly Rat is not the right sign to deal with this scenario; so in 2012, Rat is likely to keep its distance & probably even disengage itself from any relationship with a Sheep partner.

In extreme cases the differences between this pair might spill into ugly fights and involve litigations and going to the courts. Truly in 2012, it is advisable for this pair to simply back off from each other. Those already involved with each other - if you find that the year causes you to fight a lot or argue and scream at each other, it may be better for you to take a break from each other.

Spend some time apart and allow time for the feng shui afflictive winds to blow way. So maybe take a holiday or simply stay out of each other's way.

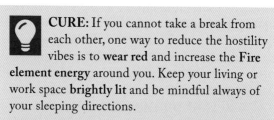 **CURE:** If you cannot take a break from each other, one way to reduce the hostility vibes is to **wear red** and increase the **Fire element energy** around you. Keep your living or work space **brightly lit** and be mindful always of your sleeping directions.

You will find that by sleeping with your head pointed to your **personalised love direction** (your *nien yen* direction) will substantially reduce conflicts between you. Or you can also place **six crystal balls** on your coffee table in the living room - placed so you can see them - this too is an excellent remedy for disharmony caused by the number 3 star.

(*A Fairweather Couple* ★★)

SHEEP WITH TIGER
In 2012, tendency to fight & quarrel too much

The Tiger and the Sheep generally do not get along and they are definitely not compatible. Their differences go underneath the skin and these are two signs unlikely to get together or stay together for too long. Somehow or other, problems and misunderstandings will crop up between them no matter how much they may try to be accommodating.

The problem with this pair is that they are really very different from each other. But they can be instantly attracted to one another in the way opposites can find each other attractive, this being one of the mysteries of relationship dynamics!

In the case of Tiger and Sheep, they can sometimes find each other suitable as potential spouse material and here they are attracted to some pretty superficial things, as they generally have a wrong view of each other and of each other's background and lifestyle. There is however, enough of a difference in their temperament to find one another interesting and attractive, and hence to appeal to one another.

Definitely the Tiger finds the disposition of the Sheep rather staid and even conservative, bordering on the boring! In the eyes of the extrovert and courageous Tiger, the Sheep can come across unexciting. Until of course Tiger goes deeper and finds there is much, much more behind the Sheep's quiet demeanor.

When they do find each other is when both sides are actively "looking" for a special something, because real effort is needed for this pair to take off as an "item" as initially, there is little natural attraction between them. But once hooked into a relationship, the Tiger and Sheep can become quite addicted to each other.

Usually it is when Tiger is a little older before he/she is able to appreciate someone as subtle as the Sheep. At a younger age, the wiles & wisdom of the Sheep can go completely over the head of the Tiger, who tends to appreciate the obvious more than the subtle. The Sheep meanwhile rarely, if ever, feels comfortable living the kind of lifestyle the young Tiger enjoys.

When the Tiger and Sheep get together, they will not really communicate much. What passes between them lacks passion and conviction, and they can even be described as a fairweather couple, tolerating each other only so long as there is mutual advantage. When this evaporates, so too will the relationship. But with shared goals and aspirations, there is a future for them together.

This couple rarely takes a confrontational stand against one another. The Sheep makes sure that there is always a semblance of politeness, so on the surface, there will always seem to be goodwill prevailing.

The Sheep is just so excellent at faking feelings and keeping a mask on. But do not be surprised that in 2012 the quality of Sheep's relationship with the Tiger will be marred by excessive quarrelling and misunderstandings.

Tiger and Sheep make a better couple when both are older and less immature.

SHEEP WITH DRAGON
In 2012, misunderstandings cause tensions

The year 2012 does not sit kindly on this pairing of the Dragon and Sheep. It seems that both have an array of afflictions that could prove too much for them to handle either alone or together.

The Dragon has more than its hands full coping with the five yellow, which can be so challenging. And especially since 2012 is a year when it also has a low level of Chi Essence. This means the Dragon needs to borrow strength from others & certainly the Sheep cannot help much.

The Sheep must cope with its *Yearly Killing Star* energy brought by the 24 Mountains Compass AND take care of the hostile 3 star brought by the Flying Star chart, at the same time. Sheep has its hands full.

So to get together with the Dragon can be simply too much of a challenge, especially since this pair, in truth, have very little in common. There is no "hook" to pull this pairing together. Thus communication between them is almost nil, so it will be something of strain for them.

160

It is easy to list all the differences between them. This list is long and wide ranging. There are no sparks flying here and in fact, this pairing is quite dull.

It is hard to conceive of them being together and dating, let alone being in love. There is little on which they can build a future together, and because neither is in any way astrologically beneficial to the other, it is hard to even imagine them coming together at all.

This is not to say that either Dragon or Sheep is boring individually - just that there is no chemistry between this pair. Marrying one another will be like walking the road to nowhere. Their styles differ, as do their aspirations and values. They look at life and the world through different lens so this will be an uncomfortable relationship.

Thankfully, the Dragon and Sheep are likely to react with the coolest detachment towards each other. There is unlikely to be any kind of mad attraction between the two unless they are thrown into a situation where coming together as a couple becomes inevitable. But even then, incompatibility is obvious and boredom sets in quickly. In some cases, boredom can lead to animosity and even hostility.

Ascendants can help

Usually if these two signs get together and build a happy life together, it is because one of them has the other's ascendant, which means either the Dragon was born in the hours of the Sheep (1pm to 3 pm) or the Sheep was born in the hours of the Dragon (7 am to 9 am). The **Hour of Birth** does exert favorable influence, making an otherwise incompatible couple see something positive in each other.

Generally speaking however, this is not a couple with much to build on. In 2012, any coming together of this pair will see regular disagreements between them. Sheep will seem too quarrelsome by half. It is a very unstable pair indeed and much better if they split!

The Sheep and Dragon can get easily bored of one another.

SHEEP WITH SNAKE
Keeping each other warm by staying loving

In 2012 this unlikely pair continues to be unable to really hit it off. The Snake and the Sheep have too much instinctive distrust of each other.

> These are two signs that should actually complement each other easily. Potentially they have much they can bring to a relationship with each other; but unfortunately, the energies of most years are simply not conducive to them forging any kind of bond with one another and 2012 is one of those years.

Whatever the Snake lacks, the Sheep has in good measure and vice versa. This could be a wonderful pairing of the yin and yang, except that both parties tend to be too demanding of one another.

Expectations can be unreasonable, and neither has the patience to endure the other's constant requests for attention. This creates feelings felt by both of being unappreciated and unreasonable. Quite likely, Snake and Sheep lack the inner understanding and affinity that makes relationships flourish.

The Snake is intensely intellectual, demanding accuracy and disciplined-thought, while the Sheep depends more on instincts and on its own creative thoughts. One leans strongly on facts, while the other tends to be subjective, taking inspiration from sources the Snake considers absurd.

The Snake is more decisive than the Sheep whose mood changes are irritating. But in the Year of the Dragon, both sides take turns to be fickle about their feelings for one another. Maybe this arises from neither of this pair being genuinely committed to the other.

The Sheep is not attracted to and has little interest in living by the Snake's rational approach, and Snake simply has no interest at all, period. This is a match that lacks affinity and compatibility according to the Zodiac system of analysing their character and personality.

It is best not to pursue this relationship too deeply with each other and in any case, for the Sheep, this is not quite the year anyway to be looking to connect with someone like the Snake, who has so little in common with you.

SHEEP WITH MONKEY
In 2012, misunderstandings cause hurt to each other

Putting these two signs in the same room in 2012 is definitely not a good idea. Both these signs are hit by the year's hostility star causing both to be hostile to each other and naturally aggravatingly suspicious of each other as well. Alas between this pair could develop misunderstandings that get so severe and serious it could even end up causing harm and hurt to each other.

The Sheep and Monkey have little in common. These signs are at two ends of the emotional divide even though they live as neighbors in the Compass Wheel. One is extremely emotional and the other very analytical. Their approach to life is a result of different thought processes so their personalities also differ.

But there can develop real attraction between them, with the old adage of opposites attracting holding true. Sheep secretly admires Monkey's quick, agile brain, while Monkey finds Sheep's indirect ways of subterfuge very worthy of admiration indeed. If this pair was involved in politics, they might even be very successful as a pair simply because there is a focus point of real interest to both of them. Then maybe they might find each other admirable and endearing.

But of course politics is a scenario where love and hatred are the two blades of the same sword and at any time the sword can cut either way!

The Monkey benefits from the style and demeanor of the Sheep, who is excellent at making friends and influencing people; Sheep comes across caring and full of compassion, being gentle and patient dealing with people. Sheep also possesses the skill of at turning acquaintances into close friends, which benefits Monkey in many ways. Also Sheep is rarely competitive, so any alliance here is free of painful tensions or hidden resentments.

Usually, in case there are disagreements, the Sheep's normally passive outlook promotes mending fences. But amiable Sheep is not so amiable in 2012! So although on balance this is a workable and potentially beneficial match, the Sheep's feng shui originated afflictions could cause severe misunderstandings that get the Monkey's ire up - as a result of which there could be problems and then we could end up seeing both sides getting hurt.

In 2012 however the Monkey really is riding high and enjoying much better chi strength than the Sheep so a match between this pair could be quite uneven. The

Sheep must watch that it does not get outwitted by the Monkey or have this crafty sign take advantage of the Sheep's situation.

Those already married to each other in whatever pairing must understand that there is great imbalance of energy between the two of you in 2012; with the Monkey being stronger and having enough chi energy to hold the union or partnership together.

There might be distractions and hiccups in the relationship but nothing of lasting damage will take place. In a marriage between you however, the person calling the shots this year will be the Monkey. This is the dominant partner in the relationship.

Not an easy pairing in 2012, but in the long run, Sheep and Monkey are good for each other.

SHEEP WITH ROOSTER
A soulmate who has time for you

In this pairing, the match is quite unequal for the Sheep, because in 2012 it is too weak to cope with the super strong Rooster. In the event of any kind of confrontation or misunderstanding between Rooster and Sheep, the latter is likely to lose out... being just not strong enough.

The Sheep is advised not to pit itself against the Rooster this year, who is not only very strong in 2012 but also on a roll with good fortune winds aiding it. The Rooster, having survived a pretty rough past year, is now finding itself in a very good place with the powerful 8 star supporting it. Its chi levels and life force are also at a maximum strength.

Rooster and Sheep enjoy a soft spot for one another despite Rooster's general impatience with Sheep's slower response; as well as Sheep's almost resenting Rooster's take-charge attitude.

It is easy for there to be misunderstandings between the two, and even when one is trying to be nice, the other could resist thinking good thoughts. But

in 2012, Rooster's strength makes this sign a good
influence over Sheep.

This year favors Rooster's energy
embracing the soul, sending out
warm vibes and creating the scenario
of a deep relationship developing
between them. Sheep responds with
equal warmth, so for the year at
least, there are good feelings flowing
between this pair.

Over the long term however, despite the Rooster
making time for the Sheep, it could be difficult for
these two to develop deep feelings for each other. In
the Chinese Zodiac, the Rooster tends to be bossy
and also highly disciplined, disdaining emotional
outbursts as pathetic shows of weakness, which is why
the Rooster can handle the more hostile, aggressive
2012 Sheep.

If these two are married, it is likely that the Sheep
would have developed great tolerance for the Rooster's
ways, realising that under all that swagger beats a
heart of gold.

In the initial stages of the relationship the Sheep's

sensitive nature could well get put off by the Rooster's forthrightness, but in time, especially during a year like 2012 when relationship luck is somewhat afflicted, the attributes of the Rooster does show through. It is easy for the Sheep then to even come to regard the Rooster as a soulmate. Even when the Rooster is younger, this warm feeling does not go away.

The Sheep and Rooster have the potential to become soulmates.

SHEEP WITH DOG
In 2012, a good and loyal friend who brings solace

The Sheep does not have much of an affinity with the Dog, and being the stubborn and strong personalities that they are, a pairing between them is unlikely to be very smooth, especially in a year when the Sheep is hit by the quarrelsome star.

In 2012, the Sheep discovers the qualities of the Dog sign and is thus attracted. Sheep responds to the kindness and loyalty of Dog, so a pairing between them this year might work quite well.

Sheep has reason to appreciate the understanding nature of this sign and reacts in a warm fashion.

But it would be too much to expect there to develop a grand passion as neither side is capable of inspiring any deep and abiding love in the other. The Sheep and Dog are not exactly made for one another, but in 2012, they will be warmly accommodating and really quite cordial should they find themselves thrown together in a love relationship or as members of a working team.

If the relationship is a professional one, expect there could be problems arising from the mood swings and volatile nature of Sheep this year. The Sheep is indecisive, unable to make decisions and tending to find fault with the Dog's ideas and suggestions.

Despite this, Dog's intrinsic accommodating nature shows through - and in this respect, the Sheep is lucky to have a patient and tolerant partner in the Dog sign, who does not react in a negative manner at all.

In a love relationship, things are easier, as here, both signs are more relaxed and Dog is quite undemanding. In socialising with outside parties however, both are excellent at keeping friends and making others feel comfortable with them. So as a couple, they will be popular and have a big network of contacts and allies. Life together can be reasonably pleasant.

Chapter Five

ANALYZING SHEEP'S LUCK FOR EACH MONTH IN 2012

The Sheep enjoys a meaningful year when it comes to success and attainments, but where the year fails the Sheep is when it comes to relationships and dealings with others. As well as being afflicted by the number 3 quarrelsome star, you also have to contend with the Yearly Killing, Yearly Conflict and Sitting Three Killings stars of the 24 Mountains Compass. This creates a lot of animosity and hostility between you and others, whether real or imagined. You lack patience and find it difficult to be satisfied, even when things are going well. Your afflictions are thus mainly internal ones which you have to work through yourself. If you can control your temper and counter your tendency towards negativity this year, 2012 looks really quite promising.

FIRST MONTH
February 4th - March 5th 2012

YEAR STARTS WITH SNIFFLES; YOU NEED TO UNWIND

The year begins quite stressfully for the Sheep, mostly because you're feeling under the weather. The illness star has flown into your chart, making you more prone to falling sick, catching bugs and viruses and also making you more accident prone. Watch out for your health, for this could take a battering this month. Sheep who are elderly should take extra care and avoid sleeping in Southwest located bedrooms. You should also wear the **anti-illness amulet** or the **Wu Lou** in gold. Abstain from dangerous sports if you can help it and don't drive too fast. Avoid surgery this month unless absolutely necessary. Schedule long trips away from home for another time, and stay away from overly yin dwellings such as hospitals, police stations and cemeteries. It is important to look after yourself this month.

WORK & CAREER - A Mixed Month

This is a mixed month for the Sheep pursuing a career. You have both friends and foes at work but sometimes it is hard to figure out which is which.

Watch your back this month, as you don't know who to trust. Things may not be what they seem, so best not to reveal too much to anyone. Instead, focus on producing good work, stay out of office politics, don't take sides. Offer a helping hand when asked; you may need the favor returned sooner than you think.

> Carry your **Crest of Allies** to boost ally luck. You may have to deal with colleagues or even one of your superiors constantly taking credit for your work. Be generous in spirit, because if you're delivering, the people who matter will notice. If you remain conscientious, you won't be sidelined.

BUSINESS - A Time to Strategize

Things could get competitive in the business arena this month, but you're not quite feeling up to launching a retaliation. Next month your luck improves, so save your big moves for later. Spend the next four weeks planning and formulating a proper strategy. Reacting off the seat of your pants is probably not such a good idea right now. This is also not the best of times to invest in risky ventures or to go into a new partnership with an unknown quantity. Work with people who've done business with before. Focus on consolidating your resources. If something needs fixing, tap on the brainpower of your team; don't try to solve everything on your own. The more credit you give others, the better they will perform for you.

LOVE & RELATIONSHIPS - Satisfying

You prefer socializing quietly this month, in small intimate groups rather than at large, loud parties. Your love life also reflects your more somber mood this month and you'll find yourself seeking out quiet and soothing company. This is actually a good time to put some effort into deepening some of your current friendships and relationships.

When it comes to romance, love could blossom in the most unexpected of places or circumstances. Go with the flow. If something is meant to happen, let it. Things will work out for the best. You're more about the connection of minds right now. Raw and physical passion is not something that turns you on; rather, you're looking for someone you're totally comfortable with, whether you're wearing makeup or not.

EDUCATION - Feeling Under the Weather

You may be weighed down by ill health this month, nothing serious, but pesky enough to slow you down considerably. Don't hope to get too many things done right now. It is better to focus than to spread yourself too thin.

SECOND MONTH
March 6th - April 4th 2012

THINGS IMPROVE AS THE LUCK OF THE YEAR KICKS IN

Your luck improves, with victory luck on your side. You are feeling competitive again, and whoever wronged you in the recent past had better watch out, because a Sheep on the warpath is someone to be reckoned with. But try not to put too much energy into retaliation, as your efforts are so much better spent elsewhere. You enjoy the promise of wealth luck and success. When looking to get ahead, focus inward not outward. Look how you can improve yourself, rather than how you can get the better of the next person. This is a time when anything you start promises to be successful, so don't let yourself get lazy. Be hungry and excited. You possess the power to enthuse everyone around you, so use this to your advantage to seize opportunities that come your way.

WORK & CAREER - Stay Confident

Working life becomes pleasant and there will be none of the politics of last month. You start to really enjoy your job and your enthusiasm shows. Expect to be offered more responsibility at work, and when it is

177

asked of you, don't refuse! This is a great time to show your superiors what you are made of. Go ahead and take on more than you can handle. You'll learn up what you need to know quickly and naturally. Even if you're feeling out of your depth, if you are thrown in the deep end, you'll swim. Your greatest asset is your confidence, so don't let that slide. Even if you're not totally sure of yourself, act like you are. Your bravado will soon be more than just bravado, it will be a newfound confidence.

BUSINESS - Promising Indeed

A great time to engage in important discussions or to cut new deals. Exciting opportunities come your way. Have an open mind when it comes to new possibilities; a new idea could lead to a most profitable diversification in your business giving you the answer to your wish for expansion. You can afford to take risks this month because luck is most definitely on your side.

Don't let minor obstacles get in your way. If you want something badly enough, it becomes easy to sidestep any obstacles. Don't make mountains out of molehills. If you give trivial aggravations too much attention, they become bigger than they need be. Keep your focus on the main prize.

LOVE & RELATIONSHIPS - On Your Terms

You are very much your own person this month and it is mighty difficult to change you. Those who try won't keep your interest for very long. So you find yourself attracted to individuals who like you just the way you are. You are not an easy character to deal with this year, but if someone knows how to press the right buttons, you are theirs heart and soul. The Sheep makes a terrific lover and partner, and anybody would be lucky to have you.

You have fabulous *Victory Luck* this month, so anyone you set your heart on can be yours. But it's whether you can be bothered to compete for someone's affections. You have other more important things on your mind and prefer to settle for someone who isn't so much hard work. The way to your heart is to reciprocate your advances. Anyone who does this you could fall for, and fall for hard.

EDUCATION - Self Sufficient

This month you work much better alone. You are single-minded about what you want, and don't really need anyone else telling you what you should be aiming for. Stick by your judgment. Take advice when it is good, but only if you believe in it. Don't change your mind just because someone else told you to.

THIRD MONTH
April 5th - May 5th 2012

GOOD MONTH WHEN PLANS FOR BUSINESS OR CAREER TAKE ROOT

An energetic month awaits you. You can achieve many things if you want, but taking on too much could take a toll on your health and your quality of life. The Sheep personality enjoys its creature comforts including decent bedtime hours, so anything that takes you away from your comfort zone probably won't sit very well on you right now. Your life is moving at a fast pace and on occasion, you really want slow down. If so, do make the time for rest and relaxation, and also recuperation, or burning out could be a distinct and real possibility. Pace yourself even if your world is too exhilarating to stop for a pause right now. It is important that you do not run yourself into the ground.

WORK & CAREER - Plan Ahead

You're raring to go and could well have had an incident that fires you up. Use this enthusiasm wisely. Play your cards right. For those of you working in highly political environments do watch your step.

Don't jump into action immediately. Always think and plan ahead. There's no better advice than to do your research and know all the facts before engaging in important discussions. You are on show this month and so making a good impressions becomes especially important. The good news is you make a particularly good orator this month.

Anyone you have face-to-face interface with will succumb quite easily to your charms. Use this talent to plant ideas you've always felt to be good. Old ideas get received with much interest from significant parties. The more transparent your contribution, the more it will count towards a possible promotion in the not-too-distant future.

BUSINESS - Lots of Ideas

Your resource luck is mighty strong this month, so use this to take your business to a new level. You are probably aware already of what direction you want your company to move in next, but what's holding you back is the effective implementation of your ideas.

You need the right team of people and the right connections to get things going, and this month it seems you have both. Chance meetings seem to happen for a reason; follow up in situations like these and it could jumpstart your journey to success. While many exciting and tempting opportunities come your way, be sure to do sufficient research before embarking into unknown territory. When signing new agreements, check thoroughly, or a technicality could arise to confuse matters and to make life quite difficult.

LOVE & RELATIONSHIPS – Stay Humble

You have plenty of passion in your chart this month. The young and single Sheep especially will enjoy the month tremendously. Expect a lot of attention from the opposite sex, but stay humble. Your circle of friends is likely to grow, and socially, this month is quite exhilarating for the Sheep-born.

The Sheep looking to get hitched because all of their friends are should adopt a different attitude. Don't go steady with someone just so you have a partner to fall back on. Go for someone you can truly get into. Relationships of convenience rarely last, especially for someone so romantic but pragmatic at the same time as the Sheep.

FORTH MONTH
May 6th - June 5th 2012

EXCELLENT; EVERYTHING BLOSSOMS IN PERFECTION; HO TU COMBINATION

What a wonderful month this promises to be. The stars in your chart add up to form a Ho To combination, something that brings a lot of luck. Things fall into place for you and you feel in control of all situations. You're at the steering wheel and you like where you're going with your life. Wealth luck is good, but it's not just about the money. You are also after job satisfaction. For Sheep who are not working, make sure you have something to challenge your mind; there's nothing that will make for a more miserable Sheep person than having nothing meaningful to do. Whether it is work, personal matters or family commitments filling your plate, make it count.

WORK & CAREER - Job Satisfaction

Things at work go pretty well for the Sheep this month. Your success comes from being alert to opportunities but at the same time not being greedy or impatient to be rewarded. You are kept very busy this month, whether it is because you have your hands very full at work, or whether you have to juggle responsibilities at home as well. Schedule your life well so you don't end up stressing yourself out. The Sheep is a super organized person as long as you intend to be. Don't let yourself start getting scatterbrained, because if someone notices and makes a comment, it won't go down very well with you. Those of you in careers with high job satisfaction beyond just monetary remuneration will make good progress up the career ladder - the Sheep tends to do well when your heart is in it. But if you've hit a progress ceiling at your present job, you could tempted to try your hand at something completely different.

BUSINESS - Taking Some Risks

You enjoy fabulous prosperity luck and if you're at the helm of your own business, you stand to do very well indeed. This is a time when you should feel confident about taking risks, investing and venturing into uncharted new territory. Don't dismiss any opportunities that come your way. Big success does not come without some courage and risk-taking. You should however remember that you cannot build an empire alone. This month, the people around you become more important than ever. Working cooperatively with others allows your objectives to be achieved more quickly and more effectively.

LOVE & RELATIONSHIPS - Nurturing

The energies in your chart are very nurturing and you'll feel the urge to stop playing the field and finally settle down. Security is more important to you than wild passion and affection, and you find yourself quite pragmatic when choosing your partner. Those of you involved in one-sided love affairs where your affection is not satisfactorily reciprocated will start to lose interest. This is a good thing, as letting go emotionally will free you up for someone better who is bound to come along.

You are attractive and feeling secure about yourself, traits that make you a magnet for the right kind of partner. Although the Sheep is usually the one who zeroes in on a potential mate then makes their move, this month it could work out the other way around for you. Let yourself be swept off your feet and just enjoy the ride. You don't have to be in control all the time!

EDUCATION - Growing Up

Your goals become much clearer in your mind. You start to think about your future more, making some definite plans on how you want to get where you want to be. This is a time for maturing and growing up. There may be some challenges that test you, but use them as an invaluable learning experience.

FIFTH MONTH
June 6th - July 6th 2012

BETRAYALS & MISTRUSTS BUT THERE IS HIDDEN LUCK; SUM OF TEN

While the ominous number 7 star has flown into your sector bringing risk of loss and dishonest people into your life, things are not looking so bad at all. You have hidden luck in the sum-of-ten configuration, so you have completion luck. Projects can get successfully finished and whatever setbacks you face will be temporary. Because your luck is not at its peak, it makes sense now not to rush into anything. Instead, step back and take stock of your position. Don't allow yourself to trust others too easily, or you could set yourself up to be betrayed or let down. Use this time to create a strong foundation on which to build future successes.

WORK & CAREER - Office Intrigues
This month it pays to take things a little slower. When given a task, don't rush in it without thinking or you could end up with a lot of time wasted. Be sure you know what you're doing. Work smart and look for the best way to tackle a problem rather than react

with your first instincts. The office could feel like a rather treacherous place this month with the number 7 star wreaking its havoc. Office politics could rear its ugly head. A new team member coming on board could rock the boat, raising your guard. Watch your back. Loyalties are shifting and you do not want to be caught unawares. Have a **Rooster** on your workdesk to protect from becoming a victim of office politics. Try not to take sides and don't be too quick to give your opinion on things. Right now you have to be a little bit cunning yourself to outsmart the competition. You do however have the sum-of-ten helping you, so whatever hiccups arise can be overcome with a little perseverance.

BUSINESS - Rely On Yourself

Avoid signing new deals or entering into new areas of business. It is better to stay focused on completing what you have already started than to keep adding on new things to the equation. Put expansion plans on hold for now and concentrate on your core business. This is not a good time to go into new partnerships. If there's something you want to pursue, do it yourself rather than rely on someone else. Make sure you stay in control. There is a distinct possibility of being cheated this month, so do be alert. Don't put too much money at risk. Keep a close watch on your finances. A good feng shui cure is a **water feature** in the Southwest of the office. As well as boosting wealth and income luck by activating the indirect spirit of the Period, this will also keep the *Loss Star* under control this month.

LOVE & RELATIONSHIPS - Changes
There could be some changes to deal with in your personal life. Something either you or your partner says or does could change the balance of power within your relationship; and when there is such a change, you will both go through a period of re-adjustment. You may have to be strong for the pair of you if you want to survive whatever obstacles you both face this month. Don't let outside parties influence what you think of each other. There are forces at work which are hostile, so the important thing is to ensure you are not easily influenced.

Install a water feature in the Southwest of the office. This activates wealth luck for the whole year, but will also protect you against losses this month.

SIXTH MONTH
July 7th - Aug 7th 2012

UNEXPECTED SUPPORT BRINGS YOU BACK ON TRACK

Whatever struggles you had to cope with last month get resolved by this month and good fortune smiles down on you once again. You receive support from an unexpected source, which helps you back on track. Success is easy to come by once again, making the journey to achieving what you're after more pleasant and less stressful. You enjoy luck from the heavens this month, and good opportunities are bound to come your way. You cannot go after all of them, so choose where you want to place your focus carefully. You benefit from good counsel now. Don't dismiss advice that is offered to you, even if you may consider the source unreliable. Take whatever information comes your way, then process it yourself to formulate your own answers and strategies. There is a lot for the Sheep person to learn this month.

WORK & CAREER - Support From the Boss

Be confident as you make your moves and don't be reluctant to share your ideas. Whatever you contribute to the table will be well received. You have the right people supporting you to ensure you are not sidelined in discussions. You may even experience some favoritism from the boss, but as long as you stay humble and unassuming, this shouldn't stir up too much resentment from colleagues and co-workers. Be open to learning new things and don't assume you know everything. An arrogant attitude now won't do you any good and will only make you enemies you don't need.

BUSINESS - Help from Influential Person

Good business is all about good management this month. If you can successfully motivate your staff and team members, a lot can get achieved this month. Don't be afraid to try out new ideas. Listen when someone offers you a unique maybe different point of view. A small change could lead to big results this month. Spend time discussing ideas and improving on them. You'll be surprised how productive making time to meet and discuss among your team can be.

While some of the plans you put in motion may not reap results immediately, they soon will. You benefit from the help of someone in an important or influential position; this is when past efforts networking and cultivating contacts and friendships will come in handy.

LOVE & RELATIONSHIPS - Delightful

A delightful month when it comes to matters of the heart. You feel much more contentment with life and your positive attitude will make you great company to be around. Your sense of humor returns and you're the life of the party once again. You're feeling sociable and will enjoy nothing better than fun nights out with good friends. Sheep who are still single could have a chance meeting with an old friend who becomes more than just friends by month end. You're not lovelorn by any accounts, and if you're still single, it's because you choose to be.

Some of you will choose to pursue a more spiritual path, taking a break from the dating game. A pilgrimage or soul-searching journey could be just what you need to feel comfortable with yourself again. All in all a satisfying and happy month when it comes to relationships of all kinds.

EDUCATION - Good Guidance

There are many opportunities for the young Sheep person to grow this month. You have a lot to gain now from the right kind of guidance. It pays this month to actively seek out a suitable mentor figure to help you on your way.

SEVENTH MONTH
Aug 8th - Sept 7th 2012

SETBACKS AND PROBLEMS TEST YOUR RESOLVE AND YOUR SPIRIT

The misfortune star pays a visit making this a less fortunate month for the Sheep. Problems you thought were resolved could resurface. An old-time nemesis could return, becoming a real thorn in your side. Try not to involve yourself in too many confrontational situations. This is not the time to fight. Keep hostility to a minimum if you can help it. You're not in the best of moods, and a positive rise to a challenge on your part will not end well for you. Some of you could have some personal distress to deal with.

Stay as amicable as you can in all your relationships. Not a good time to get too close to others, especially outsiders. Getting too intimate with anyone could cause some heartache with some long-lasting effects for the Sheep. This month it is also wise to carry a protective talisman to nullify the five yellow in your chart. The **five element pagoda with a tree of life** is a good cure for the afflictions in your chart.

WORK & CAREER - Stay Low Profile

This is a time to lie low in all areas of your life, and this includes your work life. Continue to be a contributing member of the team but don't stick your neck out or offer your opinion unnecessarily. Let others have their chance to shine; yours will come later. Better not to be too high profile this month. Because of your afflicted luck this month, you risk saying the wrong things, or have what you say taken the wrong way. Sometimes even the things you do with the best of intentions could be misread, so this month, it is better to mind your own business. Don't let gossip that gets back to you to get you down. Some things may have been said, but the way they are repeated to you may not resemble the original intention at all. There could be troublemakers in your midst. Stay aloof.

BUSINESS - Avoid Risktaking

Keep things going the way they are as far as possible. During this period of afflicted luck, trouble could brew at any moment. In your dealings, better the devil you know than the one you don't. Watch you don't jump from the frying pan into the fire when trying to solve problems in your business. Move with caution. Not a good time to try to overhaul things too much. Next month is much better when it comes to making big changes of any kind. Avoid investing big and stay away from risky ventures. Hold off expansion plans. Don't take on new hires at this time. Avoid signing contracts, launching new products, projects or initiatives, and stay low profile when it comes to the media and outsiders.

LOVE & RELATIONSHIPS - Fanciful

You may have some fanciful ideas when it comes to love and romance, but this is a time when you could be disappointed again and again. You're not the easiest person to get along with right now, so don't blame others for keeping you at arm's length. You're the one needing strength, so relationships where you have to be the strong one in the pairing won't work out too well this month. Don't expect too much from new relationships or you are just going to feel let down. Married Sheep could find themselves short-tempered with their partners, putting a strain on the marriage. Display **six smooth round crystal balls** in the center of your living room in the home to smooth relationships within the household. Not a good month to get married or engaged.

Display 6 smooth crystal balls to smooth relations in the Sheep household this month.

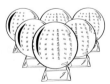

EIGHTH MONTH
Sept 8th - Oct 7th 2012

YOU MIGHT FEEL DISTRACTED & EXHAUSTED FROM WORK

The number 4 Wood star flies into your sector bringing mixed luck for the Sheep this month. While some of you will enjoy promising new romances, others will find your love life becoming something of a distraction. Your work and career could suffer as a result, as your mind is elsewhere. Those of you who are happily married won't be so afflicted, but problems for married couples come in other forms this month. Temptation outside the marriage could lead to trouble, and this could affect either you or your partner. Wear or carry the **anti-infidelity amulet** this month, or the **Rooster with Amethyst and Fan**. This month favors the young Sheep pursuing his or her studies because scholastic luck gets enhanced. A good month for self-improvement, learning new skills and expanding knowledge.

Beware infidelities when it comes to relationships. Protect your marriage with the Rooster with Amethyst and Fan.

WORK & CAREER - Distractions

Your relationships with others flourish, but this is a double-edged sword. It is easy for things to get inappropriate. Beware office romance this month. There is danger of a sex scandal, and this could come from the workplace. Avoid personal relations beyond the strictly professional, especially if you are married. You could end up losing both your marriage and your job! For others, distractions stemming from your personal life could get in the way of your work. Lack of concentration could cause you costly mistakes in your job, and a wandering mind could get you into trouble in team meetings and discussions. Work at focusing if you're serious about your career prospects.

BUSINESS - Timing is Off

You face a potentially stressful month ahead when business luck is down. You may have overextended yourself or changed your mind on a decision that cannot be overturned. Your timing is off, so better to avoid taking any gambles. There is risk of losing money, so keep a good check on your finances. Problems with staff and personnel could arise, adding more anxiety to the mix. Perhaps a good time to take a holiday. Some time off away from work could be the best thing for the Sheep right now. If you've been working hard all-year, you may need a few days off to recharge and refresh the mind.

LOVE & RELATIONSHIPS – Risk of Scandal

The romantic star has flown into your sector, so romance is most definitely in the air. Problem is romances this month have a tendency to be illicit in nature. Be sure you know what you are getting into. If things don't seem quite right, scratch beneath the surface. You don't want to get caught up in some kind of love triangle, because you could end up the most badly hurt from the experience.

Married Sheep should be more careful this month. There is danger of a sex scandal if you let your guard down. Nothing even has to happen; an innocent drink with someone inappropriate could get tongues wagging, and this could be enough to harm your relationship with your spouse. Strengthen your bond with your partner to ensure this kind of thing does not happen by wearing the **double happiness symbol**. Ideally, both of you should wear it.

NINTH MONTH
Oct 8th - Nov 6th 2012

TENSIONS BUILD UP CAUSING TEMPER TANTRUMS & FLARE UPS

This is an awfully argumentative month for the Sheep, when the number 3 quarrelsome star gets doubled in your chart. Your temper is short and the smallest thing can set you off. You are fragile this month. Work at keeping your cool or your bad temper will be your undoing. Saying the wrong thing will be ten times worse this month than at any other time. Others are not so forgiving of you, so you have to be doubly careful with your words. Don't raise your voice when angry; you will only run up your blood pressure and in the end your health could suffer. There is also risk of lawsuits, legal entanglements and trouble with the authorities. The quarrelsome star is fierce this month and needs to be controlled. Display the **Pi Yao with Fire Sword** in the Southwest sector of your home as well as rooms you frequently use.

The double quarrelsome Wood star is fierce this month, and needs to be controlled with a Pi Yao with Fire Sword placed in the Southwest.

WORK & CAREER - Be More Tolerant

You may find yourself more intense this month and will not suffer fools gladly. Others miss your good intentions perhaps because of the aggressive way you tend to put things across. Even if you think you know best, sometimes it is not what you think that's important. Learn to be more tolerant of other people's viewpoints. This month you're better off letting others take the lead than to wrestle for top spot. Focus on improving relations with your co-workers if you are hoping to enjoy the month. Work hard, but don't try too hard. Keep your ideas to yourself for now. Don't take too much time off work taking leave, and don't turn up late or leave early too often; this month, everything gets noticed.

BUSINESS - Danger of Lawsuits

Things do not go as smoothly as you would like this month. Deals you thought were confirmed could fall through at the last minute. Associates you worked well with before could act out of character. There is also danger of lawsuits cropping up to stress you out even more. Focus your attention on nullifying the ill effects of the double 3 star by displaying the appropriate cures in the Southwest this month. Place the **Chi Lin with Red Sword** in the Southwest of your office and carry one with you as a talisman hanging.

Wear the **Fire Totem Talisman** pendant to surround yourself with protective energy this month. You are vulnerable to legal entanglements, court cases and even trouble with the authorities. Keep a low profile or you could attract unwanted attention and of the wrong kind this month.

LOVE & RELATIONSHIPS - Not Too Amiable

You are more aggressive this month and less amiable, making your relationships with others pricklier than usual. Whether with friends or romantic interests, you are unlikely to make a very good impression this month, so it may be better to limit your contact with others to those closest to you. Calm your mind and pursue activities that do not involve too much discourse and discussion. You are argumentative to the point of quarreling just for quarrelling's sake. When it comes to new and budding romances, this could be very damaging for your chances in the future, so perhaps cool it when it comes to trying to romance somebody.

EDUCATION - Avoid Too Much Group Work

Channel your energies into academic work and you could turn out some splendid results. This is not a good time however to involve yourself in too much group work. You are too argumentative right now for that to work well.

TENTH MONTH
Nov 7th - Dec 6th 2012

OVERCOME ILLNESS ENERGIES WITH REMEDIES

Your health suffers due to the appearance of the illness star in your chart. You are more prone to falling sick, and accidents involving physical injury become more likely. Avoid exposing yourself to the elements and take good care of yourself. You are short on energy, making it frustrating if there are many things you want to get done. Instead of setting yourself impossible deadlines, make a proper plan to complete your tasks in good time. Slow and steady will work far better this month than racing ahead of yourself. Carry the **Wu Lou** or the **anti-illness amulet**, and also display a Wu Lou by your bedside. This will help keep illness energies at bay. Avoid lengthy journeys and too much travel this month. Also be careful if you're a regular participant of risky sports.

WORK & CAREER - Feeling Weak

You're not feeling so strong this month, and poor health could be a big contributing factor. Pace yourself at work and don't stay back late night after night trying to complete tasks. You could end up making mistakes this way, which could get you into even more trouble. You're also emotionally weaker this month, and more easily provoked. You may feel that everyone is conspiring against you, but that is most probably not the case at all. But if you react to them as if they are, they just might begin to. Stop feeling sorry for yourself and learn to put some trust in others. Things are sure to improve with the better energies next month.

BUSINESS - Danger to Your Reputation

This is a dangerous month for high profile businessmen and politicians. There is danger to your reputation as a result of gossip. Protect the Southwest sector with **Pi Yao with Red Flaming Sword** and wear the **sacred scarf with the Dhamachakra Wheel**. You need protection this month because you could face some fierce adversaries, some of them not even known to you. Not a good time to plan retaliation of any sort, but it is best to maintain a low profile for now. Avoid anything that could be interpreted as scandalous, because your reputation is what is in danger. Not a good month for new investments and avoid speculating or gambling.

LOVE & RELATIONSHIPS - Better for Men

Love luck is more promising than career and money luck this month, but this is more the case for men. The gentleman Sheep has plenty of romance luck, but women will have to work harder at keeping their partners. This is a good time for the single Sheep who enjoys the flirting game. But those already in steady relationships may meet up with temptation from outside the relationship.

Avoid illicit affairs as the aftermath will not be pleasant. For women, there is the added danger of catching some unsavory disease, so avoid having unsafe sex. New relationships started this month are unlikely to last, so those who are serious about something long term should probably wait till next month before making the big moves.

EDUCATION - Feeling Unproductive

You are not feeling as productive as usual, so better not to try and take on too much. Do a few things well rather than a lot of things badly. Stay focused and don't spread yourself too thin. Get enough sleep and don't skip meals, no matter how busy you may get.

ELEVENTH MONTH
Dec 7th - Jan 5th 2013

Good fortune returns
& things are smooth again

Your luck improves and your efforts start to show results again. Your health is better and you are back to your usual cheery self. There may be some significant changes in your life to deal with in the near future. While these may be unexpected, they will be more than welcome, because things are changing for the better. As you approach the end of the Water Dragon Year, you feel more at ease with yourself and emotionally you are more contented with life. Relationships with others improve and this includes your romantic relationships. Young Sheep looking for love could find themselves swept off your feet. Also a great time for the student Sheep pursuing scholastic achievements. Look out for some good news coming your way soon.

WORK & CAREER - Socially Adept

This is an auspicious period when you can easily outdo the competition. Your efforts are recognized and you are likely to be rewarded handsomely for them. Some of you are in for a promotion.

This will be a happy period for the Sheep pursuing their career. Use the coming month to connect with your colleagues and co-workers. End of year office parties are a good opportunity for you to forge stronger bonds with those you work with. Your typical charm returns making you a great conversationalist. You're in demand at social occasions of all sorts because you're so good at breaking the ice and bantering about anything and everything. Make use of your skill because it could get you very far this month.

BUSINESS - Exciting New Opportunities

This month is far from business as usual. You're faced with a dozen new opportunities and everyone seems to want to work with you. Your popularity soars and you are finding it great to be in such demand again. Chance meetings at festive occasions lead to some exciting business prospects and give you some clear cut goals to start the new year with. But before you jump in and commit to being a part of some exciting new project, do carry out your due diligence. You do not want to be saddled with something that sounds great on the outset but filled with hidden hazards. If you ask for advice on certain things, do take the responses you're given seriously; it could save you time, effort and money.

LOVE & RELATIONSHIPS - Wonderful Time

The Sheep can look forward to a wonderful month with love and matters of the heart. You effortlessly gain the affection of others and there will be some who fall quite madly in love with you. Try not to go breaking anybody's heart because their reaction to your rejection could be unexpected and really quite frightening. You inspire great adoration from friends, acquaintances and those who want to get to know you more intimately. You are admired for your strength and the fact that you appear so secure and self-confident. Some of you will be saying goodbye to old relationships for good. If you have decided to break off a relationship, do so relentlessly. Do not weaken and take phonecalls from exes. If you want to move on with your life, don't hang on to the past.

EDUCATION - Goodwill

You are radiating positivity and there is plenty of goodwill between you and others. You easily impress others with your intellect as well as your charm. You enjoy Victory Luck so those of you sitting exams or taking part in competitions will fare very well indeed. Display the **Victory Horse** in the Southwest of your study; the Horse is your secret friend and zodiac housemate, and the presence of Horse energy will help actualize your very good luck this month.

TWELFTH MONTH
Jan 6th - Feb 3rd 2013

LOOKING AHEAD
& HOPING FOR A GOOD HARVEST

The new year begins very well indeed. It is a fast-paced month with a lot happening at once. You are feeling ambitious and relish your packed schedule. In fact, when you do get a moment's peace, you start to feel restless and want to know what's next on the agenda. In all the flurry of excitement, don't forget to look after your health. Living life in the fast lane is bound to take its toll on you. Watch you don't burn out. Sometimes you think you have more energy than you do, and as a result could become more susceptible to falling sick or going sour on your job. Your love life is every bit as exciting as your career right now. Which flourishes will only depend on where you want to focus your efforts.

WORK & CAREER - Chance to Impress

There is plenty to catch up on at the office, with new deadlines to meet and the boss being more demanding than usual. You're not averse to pressure, so working to a tight deadline is not daunting for you. Don't get overly meticulous about the work when time is short. Sometimes the most important thing is to get the job done, whether by hook, crook or otherwise. But this is a good time to impress the boss. What you achieve at work this month is no easy task, and you would have displayed nerves of steel and a dependability not all that common in an employee. Make the most of your energy to make an impression. If you are ambitious, you really do stand the chance to go very far and quite quickly too.

BUSINESS - Looking to the Future

You have an extremely alert mind right now and it is no longer crowded with emotional baggage or unfounded feelings of insecurity. As the new year begins, the difficult energies of the past year disappear into thin air making you more ambitious, motivated and effective.

You are looking ahead to the future in all your decision making, which stops you from getting caught up in the unimportant details. Your confidence rubs off on everyone who comes into contact with you, and you make a superb boss and leader right now. Your personal wealth luck is also promising, so this is bound to help your business as well.

LOVE & RELATIONSHIPS - Fabulous

You are in your element when it comes to love and others find you exceedingly attractive. Enjoy all the attention you're getting but don't let it get to your head. If you're looking for true love, you may have to take some chances opening up your heart. You may fear rejection and this could stop you taking steps to getting what you really want. If you can over this fear, the world is your oyster and you could end up very, very happy. When it comes to friendships, this is a good time to mend fences and make amends for past hurts.

EDUCATION - Looking Ahead

An exciting new year awaits the young Sheep. You have the world before you and good fortune is most definitely on your side. You are popular with your peers and also with your teachers or professors, and you excel not just in scholastic pursuits but extracurricular activities as well. For those of you with an interest to stand for a leadership position, go for it! Chances of success are very good right now.

Chapter Six

PROTECTING YOUR TRINITY OF LUCK USING SPIRITUAL FENG SHUI

In recent years, the need to incorporate the vital Third Dimension into the practice of feng shui has become increasingly urgent - as we observe the unbalanced energies of the world erupt in earthquakes, giant tsunamis, volcanic explosions, fierce winds, snowstorms and raging forest fires. It seems as if the four elements of the cosmic environment which control the forces of Nature are taking turns to unleash their fearsome wrath on the world, in the process also generating fierce emotions of anger and desperation that elicit killing violence. Last year, the threat of nuclear radiation poisoning the world's atmosphere, its winds and waters also became potentially a fearsome reality. The world watched as Japan suffered - it was a big wakeup call!

Then came the hundreds of tornadoes unleashed on American States that destroyed towns and cities. Then came the fires that ravaged Arizona... Will 2012 see an end to nature's wrath?

So what are the four elements of the cosmic environment? These are **fire** and **water, earth** and **wind**. These four elements signify the cosmic forces of the **Third Dimension** in feng shui; these forces are powerful but they are not caused by some evil being out to wreak revenge or death on the inhabitants of the world.

What they are, are highly visual manifestations of the severe imbalances of energy that need to be righted, and the process of rebalancing causes millions of litres of water to get displaced, hence the severe rainfalls and the tsunamis. They cause thousands of miles of earth to get shifted, hence earthquakes and volcanic eruptions, which in turn causes winds in the upper atmosphere and the currents of the seas to go awry. Temperatures blow very hot and very cold... and pockets of the world's population experience suffering, loss and depravation!

In 2010 and 2011, the onslaught of natural and manmade disasters befalling the world were reflected in the feng shui and destiny charts of those years, and the revelations of the charts of 2012 suggest a need to use **Spiritual Feng Shui** to find solutions, seek safeguards and use protection to navigate through these turbulent years; to be prepared... so to speak.

In their great wisdom, the ancient Masters had somehow devised specific methods, rituals and almost magical ways to safely live through disastrous times. For of course these natural calamities have repeated themselves - in a series of cyclical patterns - over thousands of years. We know that the world's energies work in repeating patterns and that there are cycles of change which affect our wellbeing.

To cope with these dangerous forces, it is necessary to decipher the charts, analyze the destructive forces revealed in the patterns of annual elements and then to apply cosmic remedies and transcendental cures - all part of the Third Dimension that completes our practice of feng shui. To enhance our trinity of luck i.e. our Heaven, Earth and Mankind luck.

In practicing spiritual feng shui, we look to generate good mankind luck, the luck we directly create for ourselves. The Buddhists and the Hindus call this luck generating good *KARMA*... and this is a concept that can be found in many of the world's spiritual practices.

Karma suggests that we can improve our luck, increase our longevity and experience happiness by purifying karmic debts and creating good merit through the practice of kindness, compassion and generosity. These are the basics.

Thus we discovered through the years that our feng shui work and advice always worked best when we mindfully input genuinely kind motivations.

This led us to start using rituals of purification and appeasement to keep the four elements of fire, water, earth and wind balanced around our places of living and working. We discovered that there were direct correlations between the four elements of the cosmic world and the five elements of the human world.

Different animal signs are ruled by different elements at different times. Here we found that in **time dimension feng shui** - analyzing the annual and monthly charts to study the movement of element energy over time, spiritual methods played a big part in helping us improve our use of appeasement and purification rituals. They helped us to bridge the divide between the cosmic worlds - the spiritual worlds that existed alongside ours, and to add so much to our practice of feng shui. Included in the practice of Third Dimension spiritual feng shui are rituals and vocal incantations that can quell imbalances of energy.

There are powerful prayers and special offerings that can be used to invoke the aid of the cosmic beings of our space, the local landlords who rule our environment; the spirits and protectors who can assist us subdue the angry earth, control the raging waters, and basically keep us safe, making sure we will not be in the wrong place at the wrong time, that somehow we will change our plans, delay our travels or just stay home during crucial times when the elements of the world will be out of sync and raging.

Spiritual feng shui brings the practice of feng shui into other realms of existence. It addresses parallel worlds that exist alongside ours; cosmic worlds inhabited by beings we call Spirits, protectors or even Deities who have supremacy over the elements.

There are Earth Deities and Wind Deities, Water and Fire Gods - in the old lineage texts of the ancient masters, references are made to the Four Direction Guardians, the heavenly kings who protect the four directions, North, South, East and West corners of our world, of the Eight Direction Goddesses who subdue destructive forces of wind and water and protect mankind.

Much of the information related to these powerful cosmic Deities has become the stuff of legends but they are real; and it is not difficult to invoke the assistance of these cosmic beings. It would be a big mistake to dismiss them as mere superstition!

Included here are some of the easier methods of spiritual feng shui which just about anyone can indulge in without compromising your belief systems. Always perform these practices with good motivation which is to keep your family safe, and your life humming along without success blocking obstacles.

You will notice that the use of symbolism activated by the mind's concentrated power is extremely potent, as are the purifying and offering rituals. One of the most effective way of staying safe and secure in your world is to make and wear special **magic diagrams** that incorporate **sacred symbols** and incantations or mantras into what we collectively refer to as amulets.

This practice is usually referred to as transcendental feng shui and the methods are shamanic, totally magical in their effect. The amulet can be customized to benefit different animal signs directly, incorporating the energizing symbols and syllables most beneficial to their elements in any given year. The amulet for the Sheep is given in this chapter here.

Spiritual feng shui also involves identifying the **special Deity** who has the greatest affinity with specific animal signs - these can be viewed as your **Guardian Bodhisattva,** similar to the patron saint or spiritual guide of each animal sign.

When you invite your Guardian Bodhisattva into your home, make offerings and recite their relevant mantra, you will benefit from the full force of their protective power. They will not only ensure that you stay safe and protected but will also multiply the potency of your time and space feng shui updates as well.

Incense Offerings
to Appease Local Spirit Protectors

Everyone benefits from learning how to make incense offerings on a regular basis to communicate directly with the "local landlords" that reside alongside us in our home space, on our street, in our town or village or sometimes on separate floors of high rise buildings. There is no need to be scared of them or to fear them. Most will leave human tenants alone.

When incense is offered to them, it creates the element of gratitude on their part; that is when they could assist you in whatever requests you make. It is not a widely known fact, but Spirit beings of the cosmic realm are always hungry, and at their lowest levels, they are known as hungry ghosts. The problem is that they are unable to eat! They cannot swallow food as their necks are said to be extremely narrow and the only way they can appease their hunger is by smelling aromatic, pungent incense which is yummy to them.

But just burning the incense alone is not as effective as reciting 21 times the blessing incantation that transforms the incense into sustenance for them, and then it is like giving them a feast, and the stronger the scent is, the tastier it will be to them.

There are so many auspicious benefits to preparing and then burning this incense offering in the outside space of your home, and also in the inside space by moving round each room three times in a clockwise direction.

Done once a week on your *Day of Obstacles*, the incense will chase out all negativities and cleanse your home of bad energy. The local spirits will then also attract success, good health and wellbeing. Whatever disharmony there is in the home will quickly dissolve and all the afflictions of the year will also dissipate.

For the **Sheep** person, the best day to perform this incense offering ritual is **every Thursday** and the best time would be to do it anytime **between 3 to 5pm in the afternoon**.

Offering incense is one of the best ways to appease the local spirits of the land.

In the old days, practitioners of this ritual would burn freshly-cut juniper on hot charcoal and this gives off a very pleasant aroma together with white smoke which is also very pleasing to the spirits. This method continues to be used by the mountain people such as the *Sherpas* of the Himalayan mountain regions.

In fact, if you go trekking in Nepal, you will see all along the trekking routes examples of these incense offering rituals which are done to appease the local protectors hence keeping both visiting trekkers as well as the local people safe.

It is said that the more undevelopcd a place is, the greater the presence of local spirits. Mountainous places are great favorites with the beings of the cosmic world. This is why those who go mountain climbing should always wear amulets to keep them safe from being harmed by some naughty wandering spirits.

Today however, especially if you live in the city, it is more convenient to use specially formulated incense pellets which burn easily and which give off a beautiful pungent aroma. The Malays and the Indians in Malaysia call this *kemenyen* and the Chinese sometimes use sandalwood incense powder to achieve the same effect.

Use a special incense burner that comes with a handle and as you light the incense recite prayers that consecrate the incense so that it becomes easier for the spirits to enjoy the offering incense. Remember to take a humble attitude when making the offering, and if you are a Buddhist, you can also take refuge in the triple gems before you start. The incantation mantra, to be recited at least 21 times is:

NAMAH SARVA TATHAGATA AVALOKITE OM SAMBHARA SAMBHARA HUNG

Then think that you are making offering of the incense to the landlords and protectors of your house, your street and your neighborhood. You can think that they are accepting the incense and then you can request for specific illness or obstacles to be removed. Those born in the year of the Sheep can request for protection against any conflicts arising from neighbors or colleagues through the year.

Customized Amulet to Strengthen Relationship Luck for the Sheep

There is a group of **102 Protective Amulets**, reportedly first made in the Tibetan Nyingma monastery of *Samye,* the monastery in Tibet founded by the powerful Tibetan Lotus Born Buddha known as Guru Padmasambhava or Guru Rinpoche that is designed according to astrological calculations using the Chinese calendar i.e. based on the 60 year cycle of 12 animal signs and 5 elements. Feng shui astrology attributes different influences arising from the different combinations that occur between the 12 animals and the 5 elements each year; these combinations of influences reveal the nuances of good and bad luck according to the year of birth.

Every sign requires different sanskrit syllables, symbols and invocations, which are meant to subdue bad influences facing the sign.

The amulet that is customized to the animal sign also simultaneously promotes all-round good influences to come your way; it protects your property, business and work interests, and your family and your loved ones. Worn close to the body or placed near you, it increases your prosperity and keeps you safe from wandering spirits, which you might inadvertently encounter.

Amulet of the Fire Element

The Sheep benefits from wearing what is referred to as the **Fire Amulet**; and it is shared with the other "Earth Signs" of the Zodiac, the Dog, Dragon and Ox. The amulet is usually drawn as a circle and incorporates the empowering *Dependent Arising Mantra*.

The outermost circle is embellished with designs of the Earth, and sometimes also incorporates the Fire symbol because Fire produces Earth.

The Sheep belongs to the Earth element and Fire energy will strengthen Sheep's intrinsic element, so in 2012, it is extremely beneficial to include both the Earth and Fire symbols into this amulet. Amulets work best when written in red cinnamon ink and on dark red or yellow paper or silk and then folded and then kept in a suitable casing.

Worn touching the body, amulets can block off adverse forces and keep planetary afflictions subdued. The amulet for the Sheep can be made of rice paper or silk and then kept inside a leather or metal pouch. In 2012, the Metal element signifies power and influence, so having a gold or silver casing is appropriate.

We have also incorporated other powerful wish fulfilling amulets into silk neckscarves that can be worn around the neck, and these are suitable for dressing up your outfit while helping to actualize your wishes at the same time!

Sheep should wear auspicious wishfulfilling amulets as well those with the mantra of the **Goddess Tara** or with the special mantra that fulfils your wishes:

OM PADMO USHNISHA BIMALE HUM PEH

And because the Sheep has problems in their relationship luck being harmed by the number 3 star in 2012, wearing amulets is certain to pacify these afflictive energies, making life a lot more pleasant and agreeable.

The Sheep benefits from the Fire Amulet. Just having this amulet near you will suppress any negative afflictions or influences that threaten to harm you.

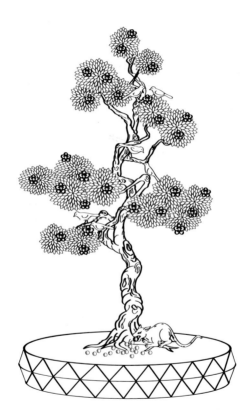

The wishgranting tree brings wonderful growth energy
for the Sheep.

226

Wish Granting Tree to Attract Serious Prosperity Creation Luck for the Sheep

The 2012 paht chee chart reveals the presence of one pillar where the elements are in a productive relationship. The month pillar shows yang water producing yang wood, and with the presence of the *lap chun* in this year's calendar, it means that there will be rejuvenated productive energy during the year. This will bring about excellent new growth.

To activate this, it is very beneficial to display a young tree of wealth that is in full bloom and which also represents a new beginning, so a tree that is usually associated with the season of Spring is quite ideal. This is a feng shui enhancing symbol that is suitable for everyone.

Plaque of Three Sheep Overlooking Mountains & Valleys to Open Up a Mountain of Abundance for the Sheep

Those born in the Sheep year can truly benefit themselves if they activate the excellent luck brought by *Three Sheep Opening the Mountain*. This imagery is believed to so auspicious because it helps the Sheep to unlock the abundance of the mountain, which contains everything that mankind can wish for. In feng shui, the mountain always brings excellent relationship luck as well as good health. So opening up the mountain, especially when the mountain also provides you the support you need to have your views heard and respected, is excellent feng shui!

Fire Totem Talisman Pendant to Safeguard Long Term Prospects

One of the most popular ways of wearing several auspicious cosmic symbols together is to use the totem concept which groups three or more powerful instruments or symbols stacked one on top of another. Totems make powerful talismans when they are correctly made and properly energized with special incantations.

Cosmic totems that put together element groups of protective sacred symbols can be excellent for compensating for a vital missing element. In 2012, the Fire element signified by the color red is required to bring about a proper balance to the energies of the world; but more than that, 2012 is the kind of year when it is extremely beneficial to invoke the powerful Bodhisattva and deity guardians of the Earth, many of whom are associated with sanskrit syllables.

The **Fire Totem Pendant** comprises three powerful sanskrit syllables - at the base is *Bam*, followed by *Ah*, and then *Hrih* at the top. These syllables are strongly associated with the Tibetan spiritual traditions and the shamans of pre-Buddhist Tibet wear these syllables to keep them safe and empowered at all times. But these syllables are also used as wish-granting aids in powerful spiritual visualisations. The syllable **Hrih** is a very powerful symbol which **protects** and also sends out a great deal of loving energy. It makes the wearer appear softer, warmer and kinder. The Fire Totem Talisman is a pendant made completely of gold which can be worn touching the throat chakra. Not many know it but the throat chakra is **red in color** and it governs the power of one's speech.

Anyone wanting their spoken words, their speech, their selling proposals and so on to become empowered can wear this totem pendant.

If you work in a profession where the way you talk, give a speech, make a proposal and otherwise use your voice is crucial, then this totem pendant is ideal

229

for you. Those in the teaching profession, in law and in the entertainment industry, for instance, would benefit greatly from wearing it.

There is a lotus and an utpala flower joining these seed syllables - and all the five items in the totem are related to the Fire energy of red. The color red signifies the Fire element. The lotus signifies purity and the utpala flower suggests the attainment of great wisdom. This is a very powerful emblem not just for protection but more importantly for empowerment. When you wear them, think that they exude rays of red light radiating outwards from you in all directions.

Invoking Sheep's Guardian Deity, Vairocana

The Sheep's Guardian Deity is the powerful Cosmic Buddha Vairocana who brings wisdom and knowledge to the ignorant mind. The presence of this Buddha in any home or work place quickly dispels all obstacles and blocks to your happiness and success.

Go in search of this Buddha Deity who was exceedingly popular during the Tang dynasty. Look for an image that "speaks" to you and then invite the image into your home. Just having the presence

Vairocana in the home is symbolically powerful especially if placed in the Southwest, the Sheep's home location.

Place offerings of water bowls, candles and food to establish a 'connection" and each time you make incense offering to the local landlords and environmental spirits, and you must include your Buddha Guardian by name, in your list of recipients. It is a good idea to make the dedication to your Buddha Guardian first.

This does not need to be a very elaborate or special ritual. The key to success in incorporating spiritual feng shui into your daily life is to be relaxed, confident and joyous about all that you do.

The great benefits of having your Buddha Guardian Deity in your home is that all the surrounding spirits of the cosmic world in the vicinity of your home always respect the Bodhisattvas and Buddhas and when you invoke their protection, it offers you safe refuge from being harmed by the spirits that may be residing in your space.

So What Do You Think?

We hope you enjoyed this book and gained some meaningful insights about your own personal horoscope and animal sign. This book, if used properly and regularly, is a goldmine of feng shui knowledge… so hopefully you are already feeling a difference and enjoying the results of positive actions you have taken.

But Don't Stop Now!

You can receive the latest weekly news and even more feng shui updates from Lillian herself absolutely FREE! Learn even more of her secrets and open your mind to the deeper possibilities of feng shui today.

Lillian Too's FREE online weekly ezine is now AVAILABLE!

Here's how easy it is to subscribe. Just go online to: *www.lilliantoomandalaezine.com* and sign up today!

Your newsletter will be delivered automatically
to your inbox each week
……………………………

You will receive a special FREE BONUS from Lillian when
you subscribe to Lillian's FREE Mandala Weekly Ezine…
but it's only available to those who register online at:
www.lilliantoomandalaezine.com
……………………………

Once you register for the weekly newsletter,
you become eligible for special discounts and offers only
available to ezine subscribers!
……………………………

DON'T BE LEFT OUT! JOIN TODAY!

Thanks again for investing in yourself and in this book.
Now join me online every week and learn how easy it really
is to make good feng shui a way of life!

Lillian's online FREE weekly ezine is only available when
you register online at *www.lilliantoomandalaezine.com*